A BLOCK

A BLOCK IN TIME

*A History of Boston's South End
from a Window on
Holyoke Street*

—

LYNNE POTTS

ISBN-13: 978-0615690711
ISBN-10: 0615690718

Conact: lynnepotts@lynnepotts.com

DESIGNED BY SAM POTTS.

𝕀𝕙 LOCAL HISTORY PUBLISHERS

PRINTED IN THE UNITED STATES.

DEDICATION

For Sam and Emmy

CONTENTS

A BLOCK IN TIME

INTRODUCTION

HOLYOKE STREET, a single block of row houses in the South End of Boston, was built in the 1860s as housing for upper- and middle-class families. But Holyoke changed radically over time, adapting to the character and economics of each new era. Generations came and went, altering their living spaces to accommodate individual needs and tastes. The houses deteriorated and had to be repaired. People made money and lost it. There seemed to be no end to change.

I bought a house on Holyoke in 1978 but it wasn't the first time I had lived in the South End. I had moved to Boston a little over a decade earlier. Prior to that I had been a student in New York, volunteering in a church on the Lower East Side where Father Bill Dwyer was rector. When the Episcopal Diocese asked Father Dwyer to move to St. Stephen's Church in Boston's South End, I asked him and his wife Tako if I could put my things on their van and tag along. I had always wanted to live in Boston and I was ready for a change.

During the next two years, I lived on Beacon Hill with old college friends and worked as an elementary teacher in the Advent School on Brimmer Street. Still in touch with the Dwyers, however, I spent a lot of time in the South End — at St. Stephen's Church and helping establish a new Learning Center on Shawmut Avenue. At the Dwyers' regular Sunday brunches I met people and got to know the neighborhood more. Some day, I thought, I'd like to live in the South End.

It would not happen soon. I met a man at the Advent School that first year and at the end of the second year, we married and moved first to Hanover, New Hampshire, and then to Berkeley, California, where my husband entered graduate school at the University of California and I taught English in a nearby high school. The late 1960s, early '70s were tumultuous years in Berkeley. The free speech movement had morphed into the anti–Vietnam War movement, then into the all kinds of *drop in* and *drop out* movements while the Black Panthers battled with the Oakland police and university students battled to keep People's Park. We were swept up in the causes and excitement, but eventually joined the *drop-outers*, packing up our books and belongings to live and work on a Vermont dairy farm with friends we knew from New York.

Our son, Sam, was three years old when we drove cross-country from Berkeley to Vermont that summer of 1973. Our daughter, Emmy, was born the following January, forty minutes after we got to the Woodstock Clinic on a below-zero morning when my husband had to jump-start the frozen VW bug with a tractor to get us on the road.

The dairy farm "experiment" didn't work out. After all the milking and gardening and endless chores, no one had time for the music and art we thought we would make, so my husband and I left and bought our own place on 200 desolate acres near lower Lake Champlain in Benson, Vermont. After two grueling winters heating the house with only a wood-burning stove, and disastrous summers gardening in vicious battles with the wood chucks, the marriage couldn't take the strain and my husband and I both moved to Boston, separately.

Fortunately I knew the South End from my time there in the early 1960s, which made it easier to find a place. Reconnecting with the Dwyers and other old friends, I was able to settle in to an un-renovated apartment on West Rutland Square for $130 a month. The apartment's back wall had pulled away from the floor (so snow settled in the dining room in winter), the kitchen sink stood on three-foot long legs, and the bathroom toilet worked by pull chain, but I was grateful to be in a neighborhood where I knew a few people and something of the city. My plan was to eventually take out a loan on the Vermont farm and use it as a down payment for a place we would live permanently.

It took two years to find the Holyoke house and even after we signed a purchase and sale agreement, I wasn't sure the deal would go through. The owner, Mrs. Hughes, had promised a number of people she would sell to them but at the last moment had changed her mind. When I told an acquaintance who had been one such hopeful buyer that I was buying #11 Holyoke, she said, "Well, good luck. I hope Mrs. Hughes actually moves this time." She hadn't on other occasions. Nor had I seen the whole house. There was a huge Yale padlock on the door to one of the top-floor rooms when I saw the house with a realtor and Mrs. Hughes told us she didn't want to disturb the tenant.

When I went over to Holyoke on moving day, there was no truck outside, and curtains still hung at the parlor windows. Mrs. Hughes answered the door when I rang the bell but only to say through a slim opening that she would need more time; I should come back in a few days. Eventually, however, she gave me a firm date and when I arrived that day, four tenants were loading a U-Haul out front. It took most of the day but when Mrs. Hughes and three men finally drove off in a rented car with the fourth driving the truck, I re-entered the house. It was strewn with plastic kitchen chairs, metal and cardboard closets, mattresses, old radios and TVs, vinyl-top tables, goose-neck lamps, scattered pots and pans, dishes and clothing. Still, it was mine; I could claim it as home.

Even though we could finally move in to the house, I realized I couldn't feel it was really my own until I knew something about its history, that of the street's, and, indeed, of the whole South End. I began asking questions, searching for answers in unexpected places such as the state capitol building's basement, the dusty catacombs of the old Registry of

Deeds, and even an abandoned schoolhouse out in Hyde Park. I visited private, public, and university libraries, historical societies, census bureaus, preservation organizations, and city agencies. Before I was done I had button-holed scores of neighbors in Charlie's Sandwich Shoppe, the community gardens, and on South End park benches.

Eventually I would learn how houses changed from single-family homes to rooming and lodging houses, and from these to apartments and condominiums. Not only would the interior configurations of the houses change, but also the ethnicities of the owners and tenants, the types of nearby shops and services, the means and avenues of transportation, and most recently the uses of open space. I would uncover events occurring over a two-hundred year history and collectively they would form a story of Holyoke Street. Of course, being *history*, the story didn't end when my research stopped. The changes I have observed and recorded will continue. Visit the block twenty years from today and I am sure you will see what I mean.

Under Water

1800 – 1850

Holyoke Street in Boston's South End sits between the bookends of Charlie's Sandwich Shoppe on Columbus Avenue at one end and the tot lot of Southwest Corridor Park at the other. Lining the sides of the block are thirty of the thirty-four original Victorian houses that were built in the 1860s and 1870s. They contain an array of apartments, condominiums, and single-family homes that characterizes urban living at the beginning of the twenty-first century.

In winter Holyoke is draped in a slushy grayness common to Northeast coastal cities in months when daylight is scarce. But on a sunny spring morning the street comes alive with a mixture of rose bricks, shiny black wrought-iron fences, and patches of jonquils, tulips, and hydrangeas in postage-stamp front yards. Windows of the curved bow fronts catch the sliced reflections of the Hancock and Prudential towers in the distance and skateboarding teens flip off the edges of the curb by the Corridor Park's basketball court. One would hardly guess, on such a day, that Holyoke had experienced such a bumpy up-and-down history in the short 140 years it has been around.

I began my tenure on Holyoke Street on a winter day in 1978 when Mrs. Hughes, an older African American woman with clear eyes and a wry smile, slid a set of twenty or more keys across the polished walnut table in the Suffolk County Registry of Deeds where lawyers had scheduled our closing. She told me some keys still worked but others probably should be thrown out. Small of stature with curly gray hair, Mrs. Hughes had the kind of determined expression and quick movements that made you know she knew how to take care of business. Months after our closing when I was tearing down a false wall in the parlor that had once cordoned off her bedroom from the kitchen, I found a piece of paper tacked to an interior surface. It read: *Practice Piano, Shopping, pay Bills, Don't forget teeth.*

Reflecting later on her comment about the keys, I realized it was emblematic of what had happened at our transaction. Eighty-three at the time, Mrs. Hughes was moving home to West Virginia where she was going to build a house for herself and the three tenant men she was taking with her. She and I represented a changing of the guard — a moment when she would leave behind her own uses of the house, and pass its future on to me. She had kept #11 Holyoke Street as a rooming house for more than thirty years. I had no idea how I would use it except as home for myself and my two young children. I would do some renting too, I thought, but first I would have to do some fixing.

When I left the Registry in the Court House that afternoon, I took the subway back to the South End neighborhood and walked down Holyoke Street. I would not be moving in until after the Christmas holidays, but I wanted to feel what it would be like to walk down the street where I now owned a house. It was dusk, and the street lights were just coming up. I stopped in front of #11 and looked at the metal storm door Mrs. Hughes had installed to replace the heavy walnut originals. Dark green curtains hung inside the windows on the parlor floor; the iron fencing that enclosed other front yards on the street was missing on mine; wooden sashes and windowsills looked ominously porous. While some houses down the block had decorative handrails, my acquisition had a plumbing pipe down one side of the front steps — nothing on the other. I wondered how long it would take me to get the house looking the way I wanted it to look.

As it turned out, longer than I would have guessed. I would scrape and paint, strip and varnish, sand and polyurethane countless surfaces on that house for the next twenty years — and even then the process would not be over. In 1997, when both my children were grown and living other places, I would cram most of the family belongings onto the parlor floor,

I.

Moving in at 11 Holyoke, 1978.

cover them with sheets and plastic, and hand the keys over to
a contractor who, over a period of ten months, would gut the
old #11 and create the new one containing two apartments
on the upper floors and a duplex (for me) below. The old

dirt-floor basement and furnace room would be transformed into a tiled office in the back and workshop for puppet-making in the front.

But this gets ahead of the story. What I really wondered that evening as I walked down the street after the closing at the Registry of Deeds was how the street came to be in the first place. When were the houses built, I wondered, and how? Who besides Mrs. Hughes had lived in #11, and how had the house been used before her? Gradually, over time, I sought out answers.

My search for the origins of Holyoke Street and, as it turned out, the rest of the South End began in the Boston Public Library (BPL) — the massive Renaissance Palazzo building facing Trinity Church in Copley Square. The library, the first large, free municipal institution of its kind in the country, possesses approximately seven million books, competing with New York City for the largest collection in the country. Here, along the northwest wall of the Bates Reading Room (with its imperious cathedral ceiling) on the second floor, I found more than 200 books on Boston sites and history. Librarians assured me that at least 500 more existed in the closed stacks of the research library. While these hundreds of books would probably never mention Holyoke Street, the long oak tables with their green-glass shaded lamps offered the perfect setting for examining what was at hand.

When English immigrants founded Boston in the early seventeenth century, the town rested on an odd, amoeba-shaped peninsula connected to the mainland by a thin umbilical cord called the Neck — at one point no more than 100 yards wide. The Charles River Receiving Basin pushed the shores on the northwest side while Boston Harbor waters lapped those to the southeast. Holyoke would eventually become a street laid out on dirt brought in to fill the basin on the Charles River side of the Neck.

This kind of information was everywhere, but it only brought up more questions. My writer/researcher friend Judy Watkins told me I should read Margaret Supplee Smith's manuscript at the South End Historical Society. It was probably the best account of the South End's early development, Judy said, and I could read it at the Society's townhouse on Massachusetts Avenue nearby. She was right. Smith's work was the most thorough and complete I would find on the early years of the South End.

The story began, Smith said, in 1800 when a committee was appointed by the Boston Town Meeting to consider plans for developing land around the Neck. The following year Charles Bulfinch, a Harvard-trained architect, submitted a landfill design recommending that the city appoint trustees to manage and dispose of the lands that would be created. The actual plan was lost over time but it is clear from other documents that Bulfinch envisioned large avenues fanning out from downtown Boston with land between for parks and large building lots.[1]

Soon, Meeting members had voted to create fifty acres of land along the Neck. While this was accomplished in ten years, unfortunately the land that had been created so quickly

2.

William Norman Map of Boston showing the Neck, 1806.

wasn't selling well. According to Smith, part of the problem was that buyers had to go through the City Council itself in order to purchase the land. Realizing that something had to be done, the Council finally decided to sell lots at auction, setting November 29, 1825, as the date for the first. Land went for the reasonable price of thirty-two cents per square foot but again, few lots were sold. Finally in 1829 Council members decided they had to do more. Their solution was to create an Office of Land Commission authorized to lay out new streets.[2] In 1828, S. P. Fuller re-drew the South End — this time with smaller lots for row houses between the larger avenues.[3] It was the Fuller plan, by the way, that became the blueprint for the neighborhood we think of as typically the South End today.

Still, because investors bought large plots to sell later as smaller parcels, land sales dragged. Jerome V. C. Smith became mayor of Boston in 1852. Determined to give sales a better boost, Smith told the Council he believed "enterprising men of limited means" were excluded from buying city lands because the down payment (ten percent of the asking price) was too great. The Council had to reduce the deposit to one percent of the cost, with an annual interest rate of five percent, Smith said.[4] After that, sales gained momentum.

While I traced the planning and building history, however, I was continually distracted by questions about the landfill itself. I wondered where the city would get the dirt with the right consistency of rocks and grit — and once it was found, how workmen would haul it in and dump it. Houses on the

---

new land would have to be built on wood pilings sunk deep enough in the dirt and mud to provide stable foundations. Where would workmen get the logs and how would they drag them into the city?

Walter Muir Whitehill's classic study, *Boston: A Topographical History*, says the first filling activity took place around the area that is now Harrison Avenue (formerly Front Street), where Chinatown and the South End come together today. At first the Front Street Corporation vied to undertake the project, but not much happened until a second group, the South Cove Associates, finally took steps in the 1830s by building a new railroad terminus in the Front Street area.[5] Landfill for the project consisted mostly of gravel brought in by boat from pits in Roxbury and Dorchester, along with some brought in from Brighton in horse-drawn rail cars. The average fill was twenty feet deep.[6] In fact, during a short period of six years in the 1830s, the Associates created fifty-five acres of land with three miles of new streets in today's Chinatown.[7]

But what about those railroad tracks, I wondered. I found the answer to that question in the basement archives of the Society for the Preservation of New England Antiquities (now part of Historic New England) on Cambridge Street near Charles Street. Here, wearing the requisite white gloves to preserve precious materials, I read Edwin Bacon's 1916 *Book of Boston* with its brief chronicling of Boston railroads.

Bacon credits two men with the origins of the American railroad. The first was Gridley Bryant, a self-educated engineer from Scituate, Massachusetts who had decided to build a monument on Bunker Hill in Charlestown to celebrate the fiftieth anniversary of the famous Revolutionary War battle waged there. To carry out his plan, Bryant bought a quarry four miles north and built a track for horse-drawn carts to transport the heavy stone down to the monument site. The tracks were laid and carts rolling on them by 1826.

The second man was a newspaper writer and editor Nathan Hale from Boston. Having learned about the new steam-driven locomotive recently invented in England, Hale fixated on having one in Boston. Strategically priming the pump for public acceptance, the scheming editor began running London stories (especially murders) in his paper, the *Boston Daily Advertiser*. Beginning with these and slowly working up from there, he finally ran a story about the opening of the Manchester and Liverpool railroad with a steam engine pulling the load. Riding the excitement and enthusiasm his story generated, Hale managed to get a Commonwealth grant to incorporate a railroad company in Boston. He immediately sent in his order to England for a locomotive and only four years after Bryant's horse-drawn railroad, Boston had its first steam locomotive![8]

In another ten years, it seemed trains were everywhere. Boston had three lines: the Boston & Lowell Railroad Company, the Boston & Worcester Railroad, and the Boston & Providence. Two of these (Boston & Worcester, and Boston & Providence) crisscrossed the Charles River Receiving Basin mentioned earlier, right near the foot of Holyoke Street. It is, in fact, the bed of the old Boston & Providence tracks that has become the route for the Orange Line subway and Amtrak rails that lay along the Southwest Corridor Park at the end of Holyoke and its neighboring streets today.

But there was more to the landfill story. Another 600 acres to the northeast of the South End in the Receiving Basin mentioned above lay fallow as marshland in the early 1800s. Uriah Cotting, a powerful Boston real estate developer, had

3.

George Smith Plan for Boston, 1851, showing the Receiving Basin and Railroad Tracks.

petitioned the city in 1814 to build a dam extending along Beacon Street to Sewell's Point in Brookline (now Kenmore Square), hoping to develop industries on a second dam built at an angle to the first along present Massachusetts Avenue. But life happened, as they say, to undo Cotting's plan: first, bigger mills sprang up along the Merrimack River making smaller ones in Boston uneconomical; second, the War of 1812, with England to gain control on the high seas, was under way; and third, new railroad beds were crisscrossing the Basin so water on the two sides became a sluggish, smelly pond.[9]

The development of the South End's neighbor, Back Bay, is a separate story — but sufficient to say, the Receiving Basin didn't stay smelly very long. Taking their cue from the South End project, a new crop of planners were soon pushing for more landfill — this time for even grander houses and bigger boulevards based on the Paris model as opposed to South End, which was more like London.

By the 1870s almost all of the row houses in the South End had been built. Maps show tracks down Washington Street for horse-drawn street cars taking passengers from downtown Boston to the South End and beyond. Soon the neighborhood would be fully settled with moneyed residents on the larger squares and avenues, and a burgeoning middle and working class on the streets with smaller homes. It would not stay as it was in the 1870s for very long, however, as we shall see in future chapters.

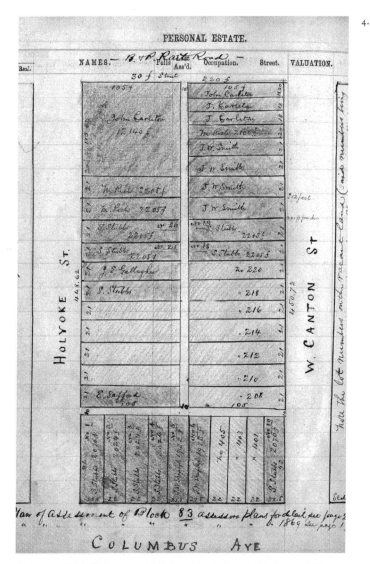

Owners on Holyoke Street in 1869: Street book page for Holyoke, 1869.

CHAPTER 2

Builders and Buyers

1850 – 1880

Standing in the middle of Holyoke Street, looking at the varying bows, stoops (front steps), and window shapes of the thirty houses that still stand, I concluded there had been eight different developers with their fingers in the Holyoke Street pie. The various groups or sets of houses (commonly comprised of four) show how each builder drew from a hodgepodge of influences: existing architectural models, what their fellow builders were doing, pictures of London streets, and their own whims. City government had laid down certain strictures (the height of the houses, distance from the street, and allowable building materials) through a system of covenanted deeds which meant the land would not be granted to a builder unless his construction conformed to certain conditions.[1] Observing the street as I did while taking notes, I could see that builders had a certain latitude for individual taste in various combinations of brick and stone choices, iron work, stoop style, Mansard slate-roofing shapes, lintel decoration, door design, and interior detail — but it was clear they had to conform to overall regulations. Of course owners who bought while builders were still working could make interior suggestions — and undoubtedly some did.

On my street one set of four houses was constructed in brick with and additional layer of sandstone slab on the front exterior. Three groups of houses have the front stoops next to each other while the rest alternate the stoops with the bays between. Yet another set of four houses have no mansards roofs but rather have bays that extend all the way to the roof line. Several houses, including the sandstone group, have angular bays (sometimes called *squared* or *flat sections*) instead of the more common rounded ones. The flat bays have a window in each of the three surfaces; the bowed have only two.

All the odd-numbered houses on the northeast side of the street have the angular bays in the back of the houses facing the alley. A few (it is hard to tell how many now, as original plans don't exist and many were changed during the condominium-conversion era) extend two floors up to create extra space and provide more light on both the parlor and lower-bedroom floor; others have the bay on the parlor floor only, as does mine at #11. All even-numbered houses from #10–#30 have rounded bays that extend from the ground to the roof

5.

Back of #11 Holyoke with bay on parlor floor.

— fancier and roomier. The remaining houses on that side have nothing in the back, a decision the builder probably made because these were closer to the railroad tracks and less likely to sell for as much as the others. Houses in one set of even-numbered houses (#24–#30) are four feet longer (front to back) than all the rest on that side of the block.

If you walk along Holyoke today you will see round iron plates over holes in the sidewalk in front of the stoops. In the early days, carts delivering coal dumped their loads through these holes to send it down into small rooms on the basement level below. When I bought my house and tried to put grass and flowers in the backyard, I couldn't help but notice that a large percentage of the soil was cinders. It turns out city workers used to bring carts up the back alley to collect these. I had to guess that on wintery cold days many homeowners just didn't want to make the trip to the alley, dumping their cinders in backyard snow instead. Builders or perhaps the city provided iron rings in the stone curb outside for tying up horses. Two Holyoke rings remain today, one in front of #9 and another at #15.

From the front, the houses appear to have only four floors but they actually have five — the last one below street level with an entrance onto the backyard. This makes three entrances: one on the parlor level at the top of the stoop, one under the stoop at ground level, and the one in the back. It's confusing when you first move in but eventually the arrangement seems not only convenient, but ingenious. Greet your guests at the top of a stately stairway; bring in your groceries at the front on the street level; and take trash downstairs directly out to the alley through the back.

I discovered early on in my research that the original architectural drawings for Holyoke were either lost in the downtown fire of 1872 or never officially filed, but it's possible to imagine what the interiors were like by examining the few houses left still more or less intact. My own house had been altered so much during its tenure as a rooming house, I had to turn to my neighbors — beginning with questions about their basements. Tom Ford, who bought #16 Holyoke in 1976, and Geri Sinclair, whose father bought #21 Holyoke in 1930, said the room closest to the backyard was for laundry purposes; the larger room in the front was for the furnace and storage. George and Andrea Moryadas, who bought in 1994, said there were soapstone tubs in the laundry room when they moved in; beside the coal room under the stoop they found a small room lined in several layers of thick wood and containing a single lead-lined shelf. Next to it was another larger room with several deep shelves lining the walls. The first room held the ice and meat, they speculated, and the second root vegetables.

All houses on the street level had a kitchen in the back and dining room in the front as far as I could ascertain. It's impossible to determine today how many, but several houses had a pantry between the kitchen and dining room that provided storage and a counter for serving dishes. Many houses had a decorative wainscoting in both rooms on this floor, some of solid paneling, as it was in the Moryadas's and some, a thin veneer glued to the plaster as it was in mine. Andrea Moryadas said she originally thought her wainscoting was oak, but later verified it was chestnut. I thought mine was walnut, but it was so scratched and torn you couldn't really tell; I finally removed it.

Every house had eleven-foot ceilings (more or less), decorative plaster moldings (commonly the egg and dart pattern), heavy solid-wood doors, and foot-thick baseboards in the two larger rooms on the parlor floor — the formal sitting room in the front and a music room in the back. When I moved into my house and began tearing up the five layers of linoleum that covered the floors of these two rooms, I found beautiful un-scarred oak floors everywhere except for a ten-foot square piece of rough-hewn pine in the middle of the music room. I had been told that this was for a carpet to cushion the piano customarily kept in that room. My neighbor Ken Kruckemeyer said the original floors were covered with wall-to-wall carpeting, later replaced with the oak flooring. The center was probably for an oriental rug with the rectangular piano under the arch opposite the mantle. Regardless, a piano usually comes into the story. The South End had a number of piano manufacturing companies and many residents had a piano of their own.

Back Bay houses on Commonwealth Avenue and other streets were built to differ from one another (Paris style) while the South End houses were attached and all very similar (London style). There's always been talk about this difference, but regardless, houses in both neighborhoods had their nineteenth-century elegant flourishes. My house, much beaten-down by the time I got it, still had double etched-glass doors built to slide smoothly into customized panels on either side between the front parlor and music room. Above my living room fireplace with marble mantle was an enormous cupid-laden mirror with a female masthead that could rival one on a Viking ship. The frame of the mirror had been painted white but when I finally got to stripping it in the early 1990s, I found gold leaf underneath.

The jewel in the crown of a typical South End house was the gracefully winding stairway that began on the street floor and wound all the way up to the top floor. Mine had carved spindles, molded walnut bannisters, parquet oak treads, and

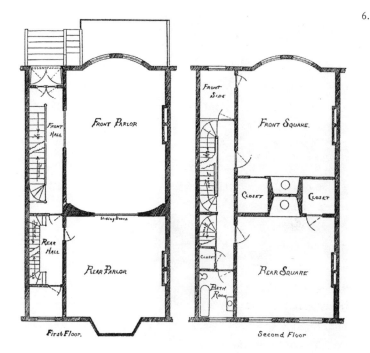

Typical Holyoke Street floor plan.

heavy decorative newel posts anchoring it on the parlor and street floors. Over the years, whenever we had family gatherings with lots of cousins around, the children would run up and down the stairway, dropping toys and pillows from the top floor to bottom, sliding down bannisters and swinging around the newel post.

When the houses were first built, the two floors above the parlor (the fourth and fifth levels) were for bedrooms. Like

7.

*South End
stairway.*

the parlor floor, each had two large rooms though there was an additional one over the staircase on the top floor. The large bedrooms on each of these floors opened on to a small room between — sometimes with custom-built cupboards, built-in drawers, and a porcelain sink.

The one bathroom, customarily equipped with pull-chain toilet, sink, and tub on lion-claw feet, was always on the fourth floor. Water pipes and drains ran along an interior wall near the back of the house. Ken Kruckemeyer of #14 said that in the earliest years the water went from the street's "main" up a pipe and into a closeted holding tank on the top floor; the system built up pressure to fill toilets and sinks on floors below.

By today's standards, South End heating systems did not provide very comfortable or efficient heat. When they were built, houses were kept warm in winter with coal-burning stoves set into the fireplace. Most of these, however, were eventually replaced by furnaces in the basement (coal and later gas) heating air sent through ducts to the floors above. When I bought #11 in 1978, it had the system that was probably installed very soon after the house was built. A huge clunky coal-burning furnace in the basement sent the heated air up through large ducts that opened into grates in the fireplaces on the floors above. The cold air returned to the basement through cut-out floor squares covered with grates in the hall-way. Practical as it seemed, the system didn't work well. Even when many people converted to oil or gas for fuel, the hot air system couldn't do the job. We could never get it any warmer than sixty-two degrees in my house during long stretches of cold in winter.

Leola Oden, who lived on Holyoke Street almost all of her 101 years, told me once she had the same problem. Speaking about her past when I visited her in a Roxbury residence for seniors in 1995, Mrs. Oden said emphatically that Holyoke Street houses were never warm. She herself had a coal-burning cook stove so she'd at least have good heat in the kitchen. Eventually steam heat with radiators replaced hot air, but many people say they never got really warm until they switched to forced hot-water baseboard heat in the 1980s. By then, a large percent of South End houses were no longer single-family homes.

The gas originally used for lighting came from a central location where, generated from burning coal in ovens, it was carried by pipes to a huge water-filled container with a cover that lifted up and down with production amounts. This large receptor, called a gasometer, built up pressure for the gas to be piped to houses.[2] The technology looked, and was, scary. To calm residents' fears, the gas companies built large brick structures around the central holding tank. There were several of these tanks around the South End in the early days. One such structure remains today near the southern end of Massachusetts Avenue, just below Boston Medical Center. During the time I was researching this book, this old brick cylinder was transformed into a Best Westin Hotel called Round House Suites.

Thinking about South End houses so much, I decided it was time to search out the history of my own. The lawyer who had helped with my closing in 1978 told me I would have to go to the Registry of Deeds in the old Suffolk County Courthouse where, beginning with my own transaction, I could trace backwards to each previous one to finally arrive at the year when #11 Holyoke was built. It took several hours but I eventually pieced together that my lot was sold by the original investor, Richard Leeds, to Samuel Stubbs, who bought several other lots as well as described on the Fuller plan of 1828. Stubbs bought his lots for a total of $7,170. The document with this information cited *Deed Book 903*, Volume 121, a cloth-over-leather tome written entirely by hand with an inside fly sheet that recorded titles, dates, and other information in seven different calligraphy styles — some with shadows and curlicues, others in classic Roman lettering.

Volume 121, shelved in a courthouse basement room with cobwebs hanging from the naked bulbs that dimly lit the room, showed that the Boston Water Power Company sold Richard Leeds a large plot of land bounded by West Brookline, West Canton, Boston & Providence Railroad, and Columbus Avenue for $43,463. It stipulated the land could not be used for a "stable, white- or blacksmith shop, or foundry." It had to be for "dwellings of good class not less than three stories high." It was more than a century later when I purchased, but I guessed I could qualify as "good class." Too late if I couldn't.

During this same nineteenth-century building period, developers were building another type of housing called *hotels* or *French flats* (comparable to our present-day rental apartment buildings). In fact, the first such hotel in the United States was Hotel Pelham, at the corner of Boylston and Tremont Street, built in 1857. Boston had more than 500 such hotels by 1890, many of them along Columbus Avenue or other South End and Back Bay streets. Hotel Alexandra on Washington Street, St. Cloud at the corner of Tremont and Clarendon, and Franklin Square House on East Newton were among them. Some included food and linens in the monthly rent.[3] At first these hotels were occupied primarily by couples or single people, accounting for the oft-repeated phrase "housing for the newly wed or nearly dead." Soon, however, they housed whole families.

One of the most notable examples of a residential hotel in the South End was the Hotel Albemarle located at the corner of Clarendon and Columbus. It's one of the few large buildings left undeveloped in the South End. Purchased by the Boston Housing Authority in the 1960s, the building houses forty-six subsidized units in spacious apartments, some with three bedrooms. I went down to see the inside of the Albemarle, and although I entered with the usual stainless steel buzzer systems, I found myself in an elegant hallway with a vast, spindle-laced staircase leading to the upper floors. A young Puerto Rican schoolgirl told me her mother had lived in the building twenty years and even though it had been dangerous with robberies and drug dealing in the late 1980s, it was "much better now."

Most of the South End's houses and hotels were in place by the end of the 1870s. While the streets were fairly treeless, it was a fresh new neighborhood with new families settling in all the time. In the next chapter we shall see who the first people were — and who came very soon to replace them.

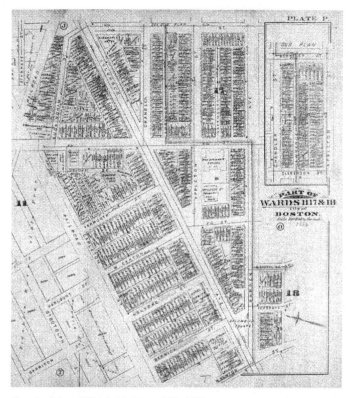

Bromley Map of Wards 11, 17, and 18, 1883.

CHAPTER 3

Change Overnight

1880 — 1900

Early buyers of homes in the South End were from Boston's merchant or professional classes, but many had barely settled in to their homes when the district seemed to change almost overnight. For one thing, the population of Boston was growing rapidly, causing housing patterns to shift. While the city had approximately 93,000 people in 1840, it had grown to have nearly 368,000 by 1880. The Irish, escaping famine back home, came in enormous numbers. There were 35,000 Irish in Boston in 1850 when they began coming; there were 50,000 five years later.[1] Italians, Jews from Eastern Europe, and others from poor and oppressive homelands were soon to follow the Irish. Everyone needed housing.

The first choice for many of these newcomers was the old Fort Hill east of Milk Street and extending to the waterfront (not to be confused with the Fort Hill in today's Roxbury), where rents were lowest. City fathers, however, had decided just about the time South End building was finished that the Fort Hill neighborhood would have to be torn down. Housing there was badly deteriorated and the hill would provide convenient landfill. Historian Lawrence Kennedy in *Planning the City Upon a Hill* wrote that it was the demolition of Fort Hill in 1866–1872 and the development of Back Bay that lessened prospects for the South End to keep middle- and higher-income families. Soon many of these groups would be moving out.[2]

It is worth noting here that South End housing built in the late nineteenth century was far from homogenous. As we have seen, large elegant homes (some having a maid's back stairway) lined Chester Square, Worcester Square and Union Park — with gracious homes on lesser squares (such as Concord, Rutland, Worcester) as well. When Fort Hill was torn down, however, developers built smaller flat-front buildings (many of them wooden) on streets below Tremont and closer to downtown. Because these were torn down in later decades, many South Enders today don't know where they were. Their names only appear in records and personal journals such as the one I found by Matt "Uno" Regan (undated) a student who wrote a paper about how his family had thrived in the "tenement" district for years. Describing this section, he said it was "around East Newton and Sharon Streets, but [including]

South Cove (where Chinese and Arabic immigrants lived, south of today's Bay Village) and the New York Streets."[3]

Holy Cross Cathedral on Washington Street and West Dedham in this neighborhood in fact failed to flourish as a city-wide institution according to *Cityscapes* authors, Campbell and Vanderwarker, because it "found itself stranded in a rooming-house backwater of the city." The cathedral had been built at a time when the Irish were emerging as a major political force in the 1870s, but it couldn't compete with Back Bay's Trinity Church as hoped, the authors said, because it was in a "poor" part of town.[4]

Other factors contributed to the shift in economic demographics during the tail end of the South End's building era. Sam Bass Warner, writing on the growth of street cars in the late nineteenth century, said these affected the changeover in population as well. Warner tells how lines from downtown Boston to Roxbury, West Roxbury, Dorchester, and Jamaica Plain sprang up, encouraging a South End exodus by making these areas accessible to people who wanted to be further out of the city with more land around their homes. As many as seven street-railway companies were formed between 1853 and 1873 to connect Boston to the suburbs.[5] The depression of 1873, when the New York Exchange was closed for ten days, also contributed to departures from the South End. It meant the city withdrew support of controlled development which had brought funding to the neighborhood in its peak building years.[6]

The changeover from middle- and upper-middle class

residents to poorer ones was dramatized by William Dean Howells in his novel *The Rise and Fall of Silas Lapham* (originally published in 1885). In it Howells describes Lapham as buying in 1872 "very cheap of a terrified gentleman of good extraction who discovered too late that the South End was not the thing and who in the eagerness of his flight to the Back Bay threw in his carpets and shades for almost nothing."[7] John P. Marquand tells a similar tale in *The Late George Apley* (originally published in 1937) when he describes how Apley's grandfather bought a South End house under the impression that this "district would become one of the most solid residential sections of Boston." The old man thought that until one morning when he saw a neighbor coming out of his house in shirt-sleeves, prompting the grandfather to put the house on the market for his own purchase price in order to sell as soon as possible.[8] And so it went.

The more I learned about this period of dramatic population change, the more curious I became about individuals who moved to Holyoke Street. Several people, including Judy Watkins once again, told me I should check out city tax records for that kind of information.

It turned out the Boston City Archives, containing original Boston tax records going as far back as 1822, were kept in an abandoned and semi-boarded-up elementary school house in Hyde Park. (They are now in a new building in West Roxbury.) At a library table in the hallway the archivist in charge gave me research instructions, explaining there were two sets of tax book records a century ago: the first, the assessor's street book with data collected every five years by a recorder who went door to door with an ink pen filling in information in columns of a large ledger; the second, actual tax records showing what property owners were asked to pay that year. It was the street books that were perfect for what I wanted to know; they contained information on each house's residents (only men were listed as they were the only ones voting and paying poll tax), their occupations, personal property (referring to the estimated value of personal possessions), estimated age, and actual poll tax. After this information, the owners were listed along with the valuation of the property.

Some books, like the 1870 street book, contained a map with color coding: brown for occupied houses; yellow for land still vacant; and white for houses under construction. Holyoke Street was still very young in 1870 with only six houses occupied by owners, nine sold but still not finished, and the rest vacant lots. The houses closest to Columbus were built first, with blocks filled in progressively as they neared the railroad tracks.

The 1874 street book showed more residents. For example, Samuel Bracket, a constable, lived at one end of the block with extra land at the back of his house for a stable. Hen Boehn had four sons, all in the liquor business. John Carlton owned the last two properties, which is undoubtedly why the cross street at the end of the block is called Carlton Street. Twelve of the thirty-four owners listed in the 1874 street book were women, nine living with husbands (occupations listed) and three (probably) widows. It is unclear why there were so many women home-owners during this period, but archivists told me their best guess was that it was security for the customarily unemployed wife in case of the husband's death, a law suit against him, or some other disaster.

By 1882, the street book showed that four out of the thirty-four property owners on Holyoke were already landlords, eight having at least one person living in the house who was not in the family. Mr. and Mrs. Lawd, for example, had two clerks and two masons living with them in #9. While the street books did not list national origins, they continued to show residents' occupations. In 1882 these jobs included: grocer, leather worker, restaurant-keeper, janitor, woolens clerk, mason, druggist, dentist, designer, clerk, shoe salesman, moldings craftsman, and insurance salesman. An actor, John Wilson, lived at #38.

Librarians at the City Archives told me I should go to the National Archives of New England, home of the federal census records, if I wanted to get more complete information. These, I learned, are in a sprawling 1980s building in Waltham, Massachusetts, which is where I drove one winter day in 1996.

It takes seventy-two years for census data to get from the door-to-door collector's notes into the hands of the general public, which meant the only archives I could get on Holyoke would be those reporting on years from 1880 to 1920. It's a scramble to find your street's Enumeration District (ED) number, then the drawer with the microfiche records you need; furthermore, it's not always productive as the ink may have faded so badly data can't be read. That was true for the Holyoke Street 1880 census. The 1890 census was lost in a flood in Washington, DC before being analyzed. Thankfully the 1900 census was intact, providing a lot of detail. For example, I learned that George Saville lived with his wife, an aunt, mother and a servant in #11 Holyoke at that time. A six-member German family and servant lived in #13; nine people from the Russian part of Poland lived in #24; more German immigrants were in #16; and a household of nine Southerners in #31. Seven of these later were labeled "lodgers." I surmised the Southerners were African Americans because, although African Americans had been in Boston since the seventeenth century, most lived on the back slope of Beacon Hill until the Irish began squeezing them out. After that they began coming to the South End.[9]

Maps of Boston during this period — both those developed for the city to record ownership and those developed for fire insurance purposes — provide an invaluable documentation on late nineteenth- and early twentieth-century neighborhoods. A very complete collection is housed in a basement room of the State House on Beacon Hill where, in cabinets and an environment-controlled "vault" frequented only by librarians, can be found early and often rare manuscripts, maps, atlases, prints, and architectural plans.

I found the earliest map of Holyoke Street I had seen so far in that State House basement. It was the 1874 *Atlas of the County of Suffolk*, Vol. I by G. M. Hopkins and Company. The map showed nothing built on the Back Bay side of the tracks at that time, but the entire South End filled in, with Holyoke firmly in place — the owners' names written in the rectangle for the property. The businesses along Albany Street give a good indication of where many people were working: E. P. Baldwin (pianos), Jas. H. Payne Planing Mill, Hinkley Locomotive Works, and three lumber companies.

While I knew I couldn't research all the Holyoke owners at this point, I wanted to at least find out more about those at #11. The 1874 G. M. Hopkins atlas of Suffolk County as well as G.W. Bromley insurance maps for the years of 1890, 1898, and 1908 all showed a woman by the name of Rosy Wiel as owner of #13 Holyoke. This caught my attention since, when I did a title search for my house, I found a deed that showed Rosy Wiel bought #11 (not #13) in 1883 and sold it to Sarah Marsh in 1902. Sarah owned it until she lost the house in 1942, when Mrs. Hughes bought it for $3,400 on a mortgage from the bank. By then it had become #11. What had happened?

It was the Bromley maps that solved the riddle. Sarah Marsh was shown as living at #13 on both the Bromley maps and on the street books until around 1920. After that, #13 fails to show up, and Sarah Marsh is suddenly living at #11. Rumors I had heard about missing #13s on other streets made me quite certain something similar had happened on Holyoke. Sarah Marsh simply didn't like the onerous #13 on her house, so she changed her house to #11 and persuaded her neighbor at #11 to go down to #9 and so forth to the end of the block, which now begins at #5. If this is what happened,

Sarah's powers of persuasion had lasting effects. To this day, no #13 exists on Holyoke Street.

Besides solving the number puzzle, it amused me to learn that all #11 Holyoke owners, back to developer Samuel Stubbs's sale to Theresa Damon and Charlotte Peabody, had been women.[10] These first two women (with Charlotte's husband signing too) sold to Rosy Wiel in 1883. Rosy, in turn, sold to Sarah Marsh for one dollar in 1902. Maybe Rosy Wiel couldn't maintain the property any more or maybe Sarah Marsh was a relative who needed income. Whatever prompted the transfer, Sarah got the property and managed to obtain a $3,000 mortgage soon after purchase either to finally get back on her financial feet or to do repairs. The reason is unclear but deeds recording liens show that Sarah paid off the mortgage by 1910. She did not live at #11 Holyoke all that time, however. The 1910 federal census showed six people living in the house at the time: Mary Maxwell, her son, and four lodgers — one from Germany, two Massachusetts-born, and one from Missouri. All the lodgers were single women in their twenties. The head of household and her son probably used the parlor and bedroom floor above for themselves, which means by then two tenants may have used the street floor (former dining room and kitchen) for their rooms. The other two probably had their rooms on the top floor. This is all conjecture as census records only give the names.

In other words, Sarah Marsh, by 1910, had become an absentee landlady. She had problems, as we shall see in a later chapter, but she held on to the property until 1942, when she

	Place of Abode			Name	Relation	Home Data				Personal Description					Education		Place of Birth
				— Ursula	Wife-H					F	Neg	30	M	27	No	yes	British India
				— Clarence R. Jr.	Son					M	Mul	4/2	S		No		Massachusetts
				— Edwin	Son					M	Neg	3½/12	S		No		Massachusetts
				Harris Fitz	Boarder					M	Neg	41	S		No	yes	British India
				Lawson Edward	Boarder					M	Neg	27	S		No	yes	South Carolina
	11	33	33	Barkley Charlotte	Head	R	75			F	Neg	54	Wd		No	yes	Virginia
				McHenry Charles	Boarder					M	Neg	49	M	33	No	yes	Georgia
				McHenry Lydia	Boarder					F	Neg	38	M	22	No	yes	Massachusetts
				Fairfax Robert N.	Boarder					M	Neg	40	Wd		No	yes	Canada English
	17	34	34	Robinson Louisa	Head	O	6500	R		F	Neg	75	Wd		No	yes	Virginia
				Winfield Lutie M.	Cousin					F	Neg	40	S		No	yes	Pennsylvania
				Morris Mirialla	Boarder					F	Neg	68	Wd	40	No	yes	Massachusetts
				Champion Estelle	Cousin					F	Neg	30	Wd	15	No	yes	Pennsylvania
	19	35	35	Newball Mary E.	Head	O	6500	R		F	Neg	50	Wd		No	yes	West Indies
				Bailey Robert	Son-in-law					M	Neg	39	M		No	yes	West Indies
				Bailey Julia M.	Daughter					F	Neg	35	M		No	yes	West Indies
				Bailey Bry M.	Grand Son					F	Neg	13	S		yes		Massachusetts
				Bailey Roberta	Grand Daughter					F	Neg	11	S		yes		Massachusetts
				Bailey Elaine T.	Grand Daughter					F	Neg	7	S		yes		Massachusetts
				Fuller Charles	Cousin					M	Neg	30	M	27	No	yes	West Indies
				Fuller Gladys	Cousin					F	Neg	24	M	22	No	yes	West Indies
				Fuller Carmine	Niece					F	Neg	½	S		No		Massachusetts
				Tomlin Rosamond	Cousin					F	Neg	35	S		No	yes	West Indies
				Cole Clementine	Boarder					F	Neg	50	Wd	30	No	yes	West Indies
	21	36	36	Ashby Pinkie	Head	O	6500	R		F	Neg	59	Wd		No	yes	Virginia
	23	37	37	Holmes Serena	Head	O	6500	R		F	Neg	45	Wd	23	yes	No	North Carolina
				Walker Melvina	Mother					F	Neg	84	Wd		No	No	North Carolina
				Myers John	Boarder					M	Neg	4½	S		No		Massachusetts
				Myers Kenneth	Boarder					M	Neg	6	S		yes	yes	Massachusetts
				Asberry Cora	Boarder					F	Neg	40	S		No	yes	New York
				Henry Eugene	Boarder					M	Neg	24	S		No	yes	New York
				Bradley Edith	Boarder					F	Neg	53	M		No	yes	Virginia
				Hamlett Ophelia	Boarder					F	Neg	27	S		No	yes	Massachusetts
				Hamlett Randolph	Boarder					M	Neg	5	S		No		Massachusetts
				Hamlett James	Boarder					M	Neg	9	S		yes		Massachusetts
	29	39	39	Chase Annie	Head	O	6500	R		F	Neg	81	Wd		No	yes	Virginia
				Saunders May B.	Daughter					F	Neg	42	S		No	yes	Dist. of Columbia
				Saunders Emma V.	Daughter					F	Neg	35	S		No	yes	Dist. of Columbia
				Saunders Henry	Boarder					M	Neg	56	S		No	yes	Virginia
				McPherson Marie	Boarder					F	Neg	21	S		No	yes	Louisiana
				Myers Lenora	Boarder					F	Neg	23	S		No	yes	Rhode Island
				Laird Elanor M.	Boarder					F	Neg	20	S		No	yes	Virginia
				Haskins Maude C.	Boarder					F	Neg	7	S		yes	yes	New York
				King Hope	Boarder					F	Neg	3½	S		No		Massachusetts
	31	40	40	Eaton Armistead	Head	R	65			M	Neg	35	M	28	No	yes	North Carolina
				— Iola	Wife-H					F	Neg	33	M	22	No	yes	North Carolina
				— Bertina L.	Daughter					F	Neg	2½	S		No		Massachusetts
				McKnight Alexander	Brother-in-law					M	Neg	22	S		No	yes	North Carolina
				Lawes Emanuel S.	Boarder					F	Neg	54	Wd		No	yes	Pennsylvania
				Lawes James H.	Boarder					M	Neg	26	S		No	yes	Massachusetts

1930 U.S Census of Holyoke Street with some houses not represented.

FIFTEENTH CENSUS OF THE UNITED STATES: 1930
POPULATION SCHEDULE

Enumeration District No. 73-12b   Sheet No. 1 B

Supervisor's District No. 12

Enumerated by me on April 5, 1930.   Charles McC...

Birthplace (mother)	Language	Code			Citizenship	Occupation	Industry	Code	Emp.	Vet.	Line
Brit. West Indies	English	00	47	✓	Na na	None					51
Brit. West Indies		53	47	0		None					52
B.W. West Indies		53	47	0		None					53
Brit. West Indies	English	00	47	✓ 1906 al yes	Porter	Building	7996	W	no		54
South Carolina		77				Colored Maid	Garage	7673	W	no		55
Virginia		74			yes	none					56
Georgia		78			yes	agent	Insurance	8885	W	yes no		57
Germany		53	13 0		yes	Forelady	Shoe Factory	7439	W	yes		58
Canada English	English	00	43	✓ 1900 na yes	None						59
Virginia		74			yes	Home Maker		XXXX			60
Virginia		58			yes	House Keeper	Home	6496	W	yes		61
New Jersey		53			yes	Maid	Furniture Store	9596	W	yes		62
Virginia		58			yes	Operator	Machine Shop	9728	W	yes		63
Virginia		12	47	✓ 1905 na yes	Home Maker		XXXX				64
West Indies	English	00	47	✓ 1910 Pa yes	Waiter	Club	6192	W	yes	no	65
Hayti	French	12	47	✓ 1920 al yes	None						66
West Indies		53	47	0	yes	None					67
West Indies		53	47	0	yes	None					68
West Indies		53	47	0		None					69
West Indies	English	00	47	✓ 1925 al yes	Waiter	Rail Road	6177	W	yes	no	70
West Indies	English	00	47	✓ 1924 al yes	None						71
West Indies		53	47	0		None					72
West Indies	English	00	47	✓ 1926 al yes	Maid	Private Family	9_96	W	yes		73
West Indies	English	00	47	✓ 1910 Pa yes	Cook	Private Family	6094	W	yes		74
Virginia		74			yes	none					75
North Carolina		76			yes	None	Nursery	829V	C			76
North Carolina		76			yes	None	Nursery	XXXX		yes		77
West Indies		53	47	0	yes	None					78
West Indies		53	47	0		None					79
New York		56			yes	Laundress					80
New York		56			yes	Porter	Building	7996	W	yes	no	81
Virginia		74			yes	Laundress	Laundry	7797	W	yes		82
Massachusetts		53			yes	Laundress	Family	7147	W			83
Massachusetts		53				None					84
Massachusetts		53				None					85
Virginia		74			yes	None		829V	C			86
Virginia		75			yes	Social Worker	Girls Home	5699	W	yes		87
Virginia		75			yes	none					88
Virginia		74			yes	Porter	Rail Road	7977	W	yes	no	89
Louisiana		85			yes	Metal Worker	Factory	7769	W	yes	no	90
Rhode Island		54			yes	Student	Oratory	XXXX				91
Virginia		74			yes	Student	Music	XXXX				92
Virginia		55			yes	None					93
Maine		53				None					94
North Carolina		76+			yes	Elevator man	Hotel	5991	W	yes	yes WW	95
North Carolina		76			yes	none					96
North Carolina		52				None					97
North Carolina		76			yes	Porter	Store	7996	W	yes	no	98
Virginia		55			yes	Maid work	Private	9596	W	yes		99
Virginia		53			yes	Cook	Rail Road	7977	W		no	100

either gave up on the house or went bankrupt. At that point, a Home Savings Bank took over #11 Holyoke and put it up for auction. Mrs. Hughes bought that year, and in 1978, I did. All women.

Tracing deeds and synchronizing sales information with tax records, census data, and map information can be a baffling process. I couldn't always make the pieces fit. They told me at the federal census bureau in Waltham that some people spend days, months, even years of their lives tracing long lost relatives or even people to whom they hope, in some remote way, to be connected. I saw I had started too late to ever become an expert, but I began to see how the chase could become addictive.

CHAPTER

4

Lives of the Newcomers

1900 – 1920

As we have seen, only a couple of decades after the South
End's bow-front houses had been built, the district had
become home to people of many ethnicities. Irish, African
Americans and West Indians had settled in significant numbers along with smaller populations of Gypsies, Nova Scotians,
Cubans, Greeks, Syrians, Chinese, Armenians, and Jews from
Russia and Eastern Europe. There were only 4,000 Jews in
Boston in 1890, for example; by 1910 there were 40,000.[1] As
might be expected, these newcomers tended to gather in ethnic enclaves, staying as close to relatives and fellow country-
men as possible. As I would soon learn from tax records and

oral histories, Holyoke Street fell into a tidy group of streets between West Newton and Dartmouth Street, bounded by Columbus Avenue and the railroad track. Almost all the residents in this area were either African American or West Indian.

As a result of both the influx of population and economic pressures discussed in the previous chapter, South End houses, built as single-family homes, soon became lodging or rooming houses. By 1885, the South End had become a lodging house district.[2] There were two lodging houses on Union Park, for example in 1874 and by 1902 there were 46.[3] Early on, the owners rented out rooms on the upper floors, but later they made all kinds of changes to fit as many people in as possible.

The number of bars, small eating establishments, and home-based dining rooms multiplied along with the new population. A 1903 map folded into Albert Wolfe's book *The Lodging House Problem in Boston* provides a key for identifying pool halls, tailoring establishments, and basement dining rooms. Holyoke has two tiny black triangles indicating houses with basement dining rooms where the landlady or manager served meals for people who lived there. These residents were called boarders and they paid more; lodgers or roomers had to cook on hot plates or eat out. The terms, however, were used interchangeably with lodging houses commonly used for both.[4] Occupations of these residents, as recorded by Wolfe, seemed to reflect the work they may have done in their own countries: steamfitters, marble cutters, cement workers, tile layers, roofers, paper-hangers and cigar makers, among others.[5]

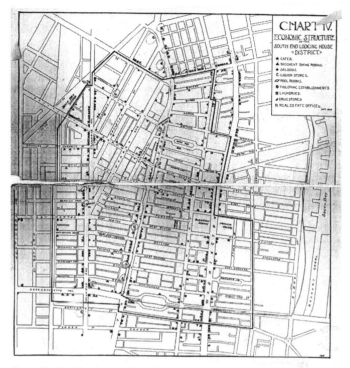

South End lodging houses, circa 1920.

The South End, a thirty-two-page booklet produced as part of a series celebrating Boston's American Revolution Bicentennial, profiles the neighborhood through the reminiscences of fourteen residents. Among the narratives is one by a seven-year-old Jewish girl, Minnie Corder, who came from Russia in 1911 to be cared for by an aunt when her father took ill. Here is Minnie Corder's story:

I arrived in Boston on a drizzly morning . . . and went to my aunt's house on Rose Street, a narrow alley like street between Harrison Avenue and Albany Street. Each side of the street was lined by closely knit, red brick houses and near each house was an overflowing garbage can waiting for the sanitation man. My aunt, her husband and their eight children all lived in one cold-water, three-flight walk-up. But their apartment did have a piano. What kind of work did you do at home was asked? 'I made buttonholes on men's underpants,' I answered. 'Fine,' said my uncle, 'we will find you a job making buttonholes in men's coats.' And so in January of 1912 I found myself working in one of the largest men's clothing companies in Boston.

I was under sixteen years of age, so I had to go to night school and bring an attendance certificate to the bookkeeper every week. The schoolroom was the nicest place I had ever seen. It was warm and well lit. The teacher was a law student during the day and taught young immigrants at night, treating us as if we were his lost relatives. I was in school at last.[6]

Another young Russian Jewish immigrant, Mary Antin, came to Boston in 1894, moving to Dover Street in the South End after first living in Chelsea. In an autobiography, *The Promised Land*, written when she was twenty-nine years old, Antin said:

We had no particular reason for coming to Dover Street. It might just as well have been Applepie Alley. For my father had sold, with the goods, fixtures and good-will of Wheeler Street store, all his hopes of ever making a living in the grocery . . . We had to live somewhere . . .

Our new home consisted of five small rooms up two flights of stairs, with the right of way through the dark corridors. In the "parlor" the dingy paper hung in rags and the plaster fell in chunks. One of the bedrooms was absolutely dark and air-tight. The kitchen looked out on a dirty court, at the back of which was the rear tenement of the estate. To us belonged, along with the five rooms and the right of way aforesaid, a block of upper space the length of a pulley line across this court, and the width of an arc described by a windy Monday's wash in its remotest wanderings.[7]

We have another source of information from this era — this from "outsiders" whose experiences nonetheless became an integral part of South End history. The story of this group began when Andover Seminary professor William Tucker told his theology students that the best way to understand their vocation was to go "work among the poor." Even more, he said, such work should not be the old-fashioned "charitable" kind but should help poor people find their "vocations" so they could eventually live productive lives.[8] In many ways,

Tucker anticipated a shift in religious thinking from philanthropy to social justice, though this was hardly noted at the time.

One of the first to act on Tucker's admonitions was Robert Woods, who came in 1892 with two friends to live at 6 Rollins Street, near the Cathedral of the Holy Cross. The men called their residence Andover House. Later Woods opened a residence for men at 20 Union Park and what has come to be known as the South End's settlement house movement[9] spread from there. By 1920 more than 3,000 families were attached to a neighborhood (or settlement) house in one way or another. These included Denison House, Dorothea Dix House, Lincoln House, Hale House, and St. Stephen's, along with several others. Some centers provided housing in addition to daily activities and classes.[10]

It turns out that Holyoke Street came to have a settlement house of its own. Julia Henson owned #37 Holyoke and had been housing young African American girls from the South for some time. In 1904, she formed an organization with friends and moved operations to #25 Holyoke, adding #27 Holyoke in 1920. Julia Henson was a friend of Harriet Tubman, the heroic black abolitionist who assisted in the successful escape of dozens of slaves during the Civil War. Henson invited Harriet Tubman to visit Boston in 1909, honoring her by giving the Holyoke house her name. In the years that followed workers removed the parlor-floor wall between #25 and #27 to make a large meeting room and recreation area. These were used by neighborhood children and adults until the late

1970s when the two houses were sold and redeveloped into an apartment building. By then several settlement houses of the South End had merged to become United South End Settlements (USES).

But again, this gets ahead of the story. During his tenure in the South End, Robert Woods got to know the neighborhood well, organizing clubs for children and establishing language and skills classes for adults. Realizing, we may assume, that he was living during an interesting period in an undocumented place, Woods recruited six others to join him in 1898 to write a book of essays on the South End. Although it sounds shockingly patronizing and prejudiced today, the book, *City Wilderness*, is probably our best source of information about everyday life among immigrants during the last decade of the nineteenth century in the South End.

Early on in the collection E. Hayes, author of the essay called "Historical," wrote, "Students of old Boston have found little in the district that is of any significance. Not much has been written about it, and any account of it must necessarily be lacking in the elements of interest which are found in the landmarks of the original Puritan town."[11] Nevertheless Hayes and the others proceeded to deliver a riveting description of the neighborhood, reflecting a bustling community with enormous energy and vitality.

Woods, in his essay on work and wages, wrote that people were employed as clerks in department stores and as skilled laborers, just as census records had shown, but he also included railroad workers and women's jobs as cooks, restaurant and hotel help, laundresses, dressmakers, stenographers, and office assistants. Altogether Woods concluded that approximately 25 percent of the area's working population were salespeople of one type or another, and another 27 percent were unskilled workers. Another 30 percent were mechanics or craftsmen, and 3 percent were professionals or merchants. There were scores of laundries and tailors lining the main streets during this period, he reported.[12]

Vendors frequently provided goods or services on credit. The South End had only two banks in the 1890s. Residents either spent what they had, borrowed from shopkeepers, or, when they had to, sold possessions for cash at one of the pawn shops peppering the district. The largest number of businesses was in the liquor trade: 200 establishments had liquor licenses in the 1890s, and of those 100 were exclusively bars.[13]

Dr. Charles Underhill, in the essay on public health in *City Wilderness*, described the neighborhood's "hucksters" and vendors roaming the streets, shouting to the windows above and selling fruits, vegetables and dairy goods from wagons on the street. There were also bakers, knife- and scissor-sharpeners, tin- and pot-makers, along with the occasional "frauds" selling questionable cures. Gangs of young men hung out on corners. Of one Irish group Woods said, "The influx of Jews has caused many of the Irish to move away from the South End to other parts of the city, but the boys on Sunday may be found with the gangs at their corner."[14]

As time went on a gang often became the core group for a club or social center established as a gathering place for men of the same nationality. A common activity among them was the "smoke talk," an affair that started in the afternoon with barrels of beer or tonic on tap and ran late into the evening with performers of comic songs, buck dancing (a kind of tap-dance done with wooden shoes), and story telling. Evenings ended with dancing that could drag on into the wee hours of the morning.[15]

The liveliest area of the South End was the entertainment district on Tremont where the Boston Center for the Arts is today. Here the Grand Theater (sporting an electricity-lit marquis) ran two shows a day with a mix of musical numbers, comedians, magicians, ventriloquists, and athletic acts before

II.

National Theater at 535 Tremont Street, 1931.

the main feature, which was usually a melodrama. Among the productions were *Two Orphans*, *Dr. Jekyll and Mr. Hyde*, and *East Lynn*. Next door to the theater, the Grand Opera House offered drama and variety shows and eventually motion pictures as well. Other night spots abounded, including the Columbia Theatre, Castle Square Theatre (with ambitious productions of the *The Mikado*, *Faust*, *Carmen*, and more), and a string of storefront prosceniums. Dance halls, drinking clubs, and trade-union meeting places stayed open for after-theater shows.[16]

"These [theaters] together with the saloons, pool rooms, all-night restaurants, and all the excitements of this street, give the fascinations of vice their full chance. When the work of the day is over, crowds of pleasure seekers fill the sidewalks; hotels and theaters become brilliant with lights; the hurdy-gurdy jungles merrily; and the street is changed for a time into a sort of fair, where evil offers itself in many attractive guises," author William Cole wrote.[17]

Cole also described the street walkers, providing details about the various types: "hookers," "down and outers", and a "higher class kept by a man . . . It is not too much to say that it [prostitution] has its haunts throughout the length and breadth of the district. No section or neighborhood — one might almost say, no block is free from it."[18]

Alvan Sanborn was another chronicler of street life in the South End. A graduate of Amherst College and student of journalism at Columbia University, Sanborn lived with Woods in the Andover House in 1896–98. Shaving his beard and head and waiting ten days for wilder growth, Sanborn donned old clothes and headed out to live among the vagrants of the neighborhood. While libraries do not know whether to call Sanborn's book '*Moody's Lodging House and Other Tenement Sketches*' (1895) sociology or fiction, clearly much of what Sanborn wrote is based on true life in the South End. Turley Street, a block in a Boston tenement district that Sanborn fictionalized, had 30 wooden houses and 30 four-story brick buildings that housed about 100 families. Sanborn catalogs everything from women's daily routines (washing, ironing, sewing, cooking and shopping) to children's games (leapfrog, hide and seek, blindman's bluff, stilt-walking, jump rope, and pitching quoits). Families kept doves and rabbits (probably for food) as well as cats and dogs.[19]

Perhaps the best clue Sanborn gives to the genial or relaxed social attitudes existing at the time are his remarks that "speaking broadly, everybody drinks some" and "sexual immorality exists here as everywhere." Pregnancy is "nothing to be afraid of," nor does it cause "forced retirement from society."[20]

With its poor people and settlement houses, the South End attracted not only people like Woods who moved in to the neighborhood, but outsiders who wanted to "do good" as well. While searching the library stacks for more early twentieth-century history one summer afternoon in 1998, I found a firsthand account of how some of these outsiders viewed their activities in the South End. Here is a quote from the *The Gentle Americans 1864–1960: Biography of a Breed*, in which author Helen Howe describes both her mother's and her own activities in the South End during these early settlement house years:

> It was to her living interest in the South End House rather than any association with Father's remote involvement with the work there that I myself became involved in a one-day-a-week volunteer stint during my winter between school and college. I have always been grateful for the ineffaceable experience of firsthand exposure to abject slum poverty of Boston's South End. I climbed the rickety stairs of dismal overcrowded tenements on my rounds to pick up children to — often gory — visits to a dental clinic. I can still evoke the mingled smell — atrophied in the air of a freezing Boston winter — of blood, dirt, and urine which emanated from the howling little victims committed to my charge, always gloveless and always handkerchief-less.[21]

Browsing the Boston Athenæum stacks for even more about everyday life during this era, I discovered the Boston directories — lists of residents during various years since 1871. (These books are the forerunners of printed telephone books.) Back pages of the directories in the early 1900s included ads for what residents were buying. The ads are treasure troves of detail: ginger ale, grind stones and building stones, coffins and caskets, luggage, skates, wine, tin cans, belts, crackers, newspapers, bed springs, oil cloth, ribbons, boots and rubbers, microscopes, urinals, corks, candy, and lead paint all make appearances.

Changes in transportation made people during this era more mobile — and the city livelier in general. Street cars, drawn by horses in the 1850s, were converted to run on electric wires strung above the tracks. The Metropolitan Railroad going from Scollay Square downtown to Roxbury began operating in 1856 putting the South End in close touch with downtown and points further southwest.[22] The trolleys undoubtedly made the neighborhood feel busier and more fast-moving. And, as we shall see in the next chapter, things were not going to slow down again for a long time.

CHAPTER

5

The Golden Years

1920 — 1950

A large photograph on the wall of Charlie's Sandwich Shoppe shows paraders marching down Columbus Avenue in a gala celebration of Boston's Tri-Centennial. The Savoy Hotel in the background is draped in red, white, and blue bunting, with people crowding the sidewalks, store entrances, and window ledges. Most of those on the sidewalks are men in suits and top hats. Women looking out of the windows from above are wearing fancy dresses and bonnets. Almost all of the onlookers are dark-skinned.

The newcomers described in the previous chapter continued to come into the South End in the early decades of the twentieth century. Those who settled on Holyoke and neighboring

12.

Boston Tricentennial parade coming up Columbus from downtown Boston, 1930, with the "Eat" sign at Charlie's Sandwich Shoppe on the corner of Columbus and Holyoke.

streets between Columbus and the railroad tracks, as we have seen, were mostly African Americans or West Indians. Some of them were still around when I began my research on the decades of the 1920s through 1950s. Almost everyone I spoke to said these were years of great neighborhood solidarity — shared poverty, yes, but shared pride, dreams, and ambitions. Many liked to call them the golden years of the South End.

Ena Harris of Braddock Park, one block over from Holyoke, was one who remembered those years. She had lived in the neighborhood almost all of her life, her Jamaican parents having come to Boston to raise a family after first settling in Canada. When I talked to Ena in the summer of 1999 she said, not wishing to reveal her exact age, that she had been in her house at 21 Braddock Park since she was a little girl. Attending the neighborhood Rice School (a corner building at Dartmouth and Appleton Streets, now converted to condominiums), and then Girls High School on West Newton Street, Ena said her memories of the decades described in this chapter were almost entirely happy ones. "It was a real neighborhood in those days. It was stable. People didn't move in and out. There were lots of big families then too. The Alexander family next to us had seven kids," she recalled.

Mr. Lynch from Barbados also lived on Braddock Park and had a tailor shop on the street floor. Lynch wasn't a great tailor, Ena said, but everyone took their things to him. The porters went to Lynch to get their uniforms mended for work on the trains. He had a high profile in the neighborhood, as did Mr. Russell, who rented bicycles on the street. Russell would take discards, fix them, and lease them for a quarter a day to children who didn't have their own.

As a little girl, Ena was a member of a club called the Smart Set that met at the Harriet Tubman House on Holyoke Street. That club, and later the "Forum" of the Women's Service Club, were formative experiences for Ena. Forum members discussed topics of the day, she recalled. "We were interested in the issues of the times. It wasn't like the kids today. We wanted to get ahead. The main concern of blacks in the neighborhood was to get the children educated."

Ena Harris thought I should talk to Myra McAdoo to learn more about South End social life during the 1930s and 1940s. Myra hadn't lived in the South End for any extended period of time so I had to track her down by telephone, but she was eager to talk and happy to come to meet me at my house. As soon as we were together she told me she identified with the South End her whole life, mostly because of her association with the clubs that Ena Harris talked about. As the daughter of the glamorous singer and socialite Gladys McAdoo, Myra spent much of her childhood and youth in classy black social circles of the time — participating in fund-raising productions at the Women's Service Club, attending parties, and preparing for the annual cotillion balls at local hotels.

Myra came from a famous family of means. Her paternal grandparents were Martha Allen McAdoo and Orpheus McAdoo, accomplished musicians who had traveled and entertained all over the world — Australia, the Far East, Europe, and Africa. Orpheus McAdoo was the producer of the Jubilee Singing Group credited with introducing Gospel music in Europe.[1] While traveling in South Africa, the McAdoos invested in diamond and gold mines, the returns of which Martha (known as Mattie) later invested in stocks and property. Although she lost much of her fortune in the market crash of 1929, Martha McAdoo owned as many as fifty houses in the South End at one time.

In *The Other Brahmins: Boston's Black Upper Class 1750–1950*, author Adelaide Cromwell relied on extensive research and interviews with forty-five women from six "Negro" women's clubs to describe the lives of blacks in Boston during this period. Cromwell cites 1914 as the year African Americans began coming in great numbers from the South, and says the West Indians, especially those from Jamaica and Barbados, came soon after. Of the nearly 12,000 blacks employed in Boston in 1940, Cromwell reports, twenty were physicians, seventeen were lawyers, twenty-nine were teachers, and seventeen were dentists, suggesting higher education levels and higher incomes.[2] Black South Enders, while close-knit and neighborly, were very conscious of social class among themselves," Myra said.

When I began inquiring about this period on Holyoke Street, Virginia Glennon of #18 Holyoke, who in the 1960s was one of the first Caucasians to buy on Holyoke, told me I should talk to her old friend Harold Hill. He had an excellent memory, she said, and had grown up in his grandmother's house at #24. "We could go to visit him on Martha's Vineyard," she said, offering to get in touch with Harold. Booking ferry passage for us soon after, Virginia took me to meet Harold where he lived in Oak Bluffs and worked as a Clerk of the Court and an artist. Following Harold around an art fair where he sold his paintings, and then joining him at an Oak Bluffs pier while he fished, I probed his memory for details about Holyoke Street.

Harold was born in 1935, moving with his family to Holyoke in 1938. He is the grandson of Rosalie Porter, a West Canton Street resident who managed a rooming house so successfully that she was able to buy a house of her own.

The fact that a Boston bank would give Mrs. Porter a loan was recognized as a singular achievement in the neighborhood since, as Harold pointed out, banks rarely loaned money to blacks — much less to black women. Recalling how his grandmother and mother rented out every room in the house except their living quarters on the street floor and one small space on the parlor floor, Harold said they turned #24 Holyoke into a flourishing business. As many as nineteen men would be sleeping in the house at one time — each paying between three and five dollars a night. Most of the roomers were cooks or waiters on the railroads.

Harold echoed others when he said the South End was a lively place in those days. People were constantly out on the stoops, in and out of their houses, or up and down Columbus Avenue running errands. Occasional trucks brought coal or ice for iceboxes, but very little traffic bothered children at play in the street. Only three people on Holyoke owned cars: Bill Brown, the Holders, and Mrs. Williamson. Harold used to ride his bicycle with attached wagon to the Boston Customs House downtown on Sunday morning to pick up the *Record American*, *Boston Globe*, *Boston Post*, and *Boston Herald*. Loading the papers into the wagon, he would return to deliver them on Holyoke for the week's pocket money.

When the New York jazz celebrities started coming to Boston, Harold said, "that's when things got really lively." As blacks, they were not permitted to stay in downtown hotels, so the musicians stayed in houses of the South End. The Holders, owners of #9 Holyoke, were particularly popular hosts. Mr. and Mrs. Holder ran a small restaurant on the street floor to feed these guests; Charlie's Sandwich Shoppe stayed open twenty-four hours a day for the same reason. After the musicians were finished playing at the Hard Hat (corner of Columbus and Massachusetts Avenue), they would come to places like the Holders' and Charlie's for platters of ribs, greens, and mashed potatoes.

Myra told me that the Bostonian Hotel off Massachusetts Avenue near the Fenway was the only hotel that welcomed blacks. A twenty-six-room upscale residence owned by Louis Cohen, the hotel opened its doors to almost all the successful artists of the period. Myra had worked at the hotel when she was in her teens and she listed people for me she remembered seeing: Sarah Vaughan, Della Reese, Carmen McCrae, Miles Davis, Stan Kenton, Ella Fitzgerald, Charlie Parker, Count Basie, Duke Ellington, George Shearing, Billy Eckstine, Nina Simone, Dionne Warwick, and Johnny Mathis — to mention just a few.

The clubs where the musicians played included Estelle's, the Pioneer Club (both off Tremont in Lower Roxbury), the High Hat (where the United South End Settlements stands today), Wally's and Morley's (on Massachusetts Avenue), and the Savoy Hotel on Columbus. Other popular spots were the Rainbow Club, the Garnet Lounge, and Louis's. The one mentioned most often is the High Hat — a fancy night spot with Art Deco interior and furnishings, a stage on the second floor, and a small area for dancing. When I asked native-born Holyoke Streeter Geri Sinclair what she remembered of the

High Hat, she dropped her customary resistance to talking and broke into a wide smile. "Oh, I went to the High Hat myself a few times," she said. "Everybody went to the High Hat."

One afternoon Louis Armstrong was practicing in one of the houses on Holyoke, probably at the Holders. Harold Hill and a group of boys were sitting outside on the stoop and eventually Armstrong came down from upstairs, sat on the steps, and started playing for the group. Another time Harold and friends were drinking beer in the basement of the High Hat where people were who didn't have money to go upstairs.

13.

Hi-Hat at 572 Columbus Avenue at Massachusetts Avenue, 1946–47.

When a well-dressed woman came in with two dogs, Harold offered to help her get them up the stairs. She thanked him politely and gave him some money so he could go upstairs to the show. The woman, Harold learned later that evening, was Billie Holiday.

A great deal of the rest of the "outdoor life" was related in one way or another to prostitution and gambling. Holyoke Street had five houses that kept prostitutes — one managed by a large formidable woman named Frankie, and two by a Mrs. Williamson. Harold and his friends used to sit on the steps and take soft drinks or chocolate-bar bets on which woman had the most men during a single evening.

Arthur Cook, known affectionately as Cookie, was born in the South End in 1908. He grew up on Shawmut Avenue, but as an adult spent most of his time around Holyoke where he controlled the numbers games played in the clubs and on the street. Arthur Manjorides, co-owner of Charlie's Sandwich Shoppe, told me that Cookie made so much money it wasn't safe for him to go home at night. Shrewdly betting on everything from dice to horses, Cookie was rich of course, but dapper and imperious as well. One time when seeing someone trying to get away with a stolen fender in a parking lot across the street from Charlie's, Cookie made the thief pay him for the loot. Cookie collected fees for parking on the lot too, though he didn't own it. It was typical, Manjorides said.

Virginia Glennon and I went to visit Cookie in 1996. He was living in a small subsidized apartment for elderly people at the corner of St. Botolph and Follen Streets. His eyes were gray and fuzzy, his chest sunken and thin, and his teeth were yellow and worn down to short stubs when he spoke. Although he was legally blind by then, he told Virginia that she looked wonderful. "She's one of my favorite people, you know," he said, adding that he was something of a ladies' man in his day. Did we know what that meant? Arthur Manjorides at Charlie's Sandwich Shoppe told me that one of Cookie's favorite maxims was, "Why stay with just one when you can make so many others happy too?"

Settling into his worn vinyl recliner by the window, Cookie recalled the heydays of Holyoke Street. Everything to do with numbers was controlled by Skeeter, Cookie said, but he himself controlled gambling — mostly dice and cards. Officially Cookie had a small food market next to a shoe repair on Columbus, just down from Charlie's Sandwich Shoppe, but this is what he said about his real job:

> Well, I'll start this way. We used to have our card games in a lot behind the gas station at the corner of Holyoke and Columbus. We had our games and the girls would be on the next block between Holyoke and West Canton. There was a place called the Monterey Club and girls used to hustle out there . . . Sometimes the card games were right on the street but I'd see that everyone paid me. Let's say I got a piece of the action. Nice people from out of town came to play with us but I'd say they couldn't

run anything without me. See, I'd shake hands with the police and hand them the money, so that way there was no trouble. The only way you had trouble was if you got a tough police. One cop out there used to hate my guts, but I knew the ropes.

Cookie said the "girls" were very professional in those days, rarely stealing from clients. Most worked the Columbus block between Holyoke Street and West Canton, using a specific locality so they were easy to find. "Men had the gambling, but the women definitely did not stay behind closed doors."

Arthur Manjorides also remembered Specs O'Keefe, a Charlie's regular who lived at the Braddock Hotel and was in on the Brinks robbery of 1950. The New York mob suspected Specs of leaking information on the job and sent a hit man named Trigger to shoot him. Trigger's aim was bad and Specs survived, but a Boston traffic cop recognized Trigger later and he was eventually hung for that and other crimes. Specs lived and stayed in the neighborhood until he died of natural causes years later, Arthur said.

Harold Hill remembers thirteen different bars on the five Columbus Avenue blocks that ran between West Newton and Dartmouth Streets. "Black men drank all the time," he said. "They don't have the same criteria for alcoholism that white people do. Every Friday and Saturday they partied all day and drank." Alcoholism was a social escape, Harold said, and not just for the men. The mothers and older women in the neighborhood felt confined, and many addressed the sadness and monotony by drinking. Both his mother and grandmother drank a lot, he said. When I moved to Holyoke Street I met Harold's mother, then an elderly woman. I remember her sitting outside on a chair near her street-level door, greeting people with a drowsy smile as they walked by.

Few adults who lived on Holyoke during these decades ever went far out of the neighborhood. Harold and his friends did so noticeably more than teenagers from nearby neighborhoods. When he was at Northeastern University a couple of years after serving in the army, Harold wrote a paper on the daily travel patterns of neighborhood adults. He found that few people ever went further than three blocks from home for their groceries. It didn't matter what a store carried. "People always went to the closest place. The idea was, you didn't go outside of where you were. A lot of the kids wouldn't even go away for higher education. They had the mentality to stay close to home."

The market for Holyoke Street was Rosen's, a convenience grocery store on Columbus between Yarmouth and West Canton. Harold Hill worked at Rosen's from 3:00 P.M. to 7:00 P.M. and all day Saturday from age thirteen to twenty. No one got to know the Rosens very well but they extended credit to buyers and everyone appreciated that. Harold used to watch Mr. Rosen throw steaks away when they had passed the sale date. Going back after the store was closed at night, he would get the discarded steaks out of the dumpster and take them home to the family. Harold also worked for Mr. Benbury, who sold ice in blocks, kerosene in five-gallon jugs, and coal by the fifty-pound bag. When I moved to Holyoke in 1978 and inquired about an oil company, everyone I spoke to suggested Mr. Benbury. It was he who would faithfully pull up on Holyoke Street for the next decade and fill our empty tank until I finally switched to gas in the late 1980s.

George Robinson, Geri Sinclair, Ena Harris, Harold Hill, Larkin Coleman (all from Holyoke black families) and almost everyone else who was anywhere near Holyoke Street during these years spoke highly of Tubman House. It was the place where most children made their first potholders for Mother's Day, where teens took music lessons or hung around after school, and where young and old alike came for Friday night movies. Its primary value, however, according to Harold Hill, was "putting black kids in touch with their history." Black leaders spent time at the Tubman House. "I remember Harriet Tubman's daughter came there once. There were black books to read and songs to sing. The Harriet Tubman House supported the African American Movement. I learned about Marcus Garvey at the Harriet Tubman House." Harold said he also remembers seeing Malcolm X when he was pimping in the Massachusetts Avenue area. Louis Wolcott Farrakhan was his schoolmate at English High. "Farrakhan was always neat and organized," Harold said, "very controlled and never in trouble. He was like a cat."

A. Philip Randolph, founding president of the Brotherhood of Sleeping Car Porters in 1925 and major force for desegregating defense industries and federal bureaus during the Roosevelt era, was also a frequent visitor to the South End during this period. He used to meet with neighborhood railroad workers in a room above Charlie's Sandwich Shoppe to discuss how blacks could gain fair treatment from the Pullman Company. As a reminder of this, the city placed a large bronze statue of Randolph in the center of the Amtrak station at Back Bay Station on Dartmouth Street. Surrounding it are plaques on the wall with quotes by retired railroad workers. One by A. Theron Brown reads, "Being a porter was educational because of the traveling. And it was a clean job. You had your nice uniform, white shirt, and black tie. And, well, you felt like an executive. I served famous people like the Rockefeller family, the old man Rockefeller. And I had Jackie Robinson too."

CHAPTER

6

Aging Buildings

1950 – 1960

The lively social life of the golden years persisted up into the late 1950s and early 1960s, but houses and other properties suffered wear and tear that owners didn't or couldn't always address, and this began to affect all aspects of daily life. I could see in records I traced at the Boston Building Inspections Department on Massachusetts Avenue that many homeowners were cited for deteriorated brick fronts, leaky roofs, and various fire hazards. One homeowner at #20 Holyoke was cited for a falling cornice, and the owner at #30 for loose bricks. Charred roof rafters caused by an aging and dysfunctional chimney led to a citation for #5. Several owners were warned they needed to replace plaster and lathe over basement furnaces to prevent fires.

Sarah Marsh, owner of my Holyoke house in the 1920s and

1930s, was cited for operating a lodging house registered as a two-family domicile. She emphatically rejected the charge in an undated letter preserved in the Inspection Department's #11 folder which read:

> The enclosed statement of number of lodgers in 11 Holyoke Street Boston is absolutely untrue. Several years ago this house was let to the family now occupying it as a home for themselves and not as a lodging house. The[y] have lived up to the letter since as I have stated before. [They] took only two of their people with them. You speak of the sign *To Let* being in the window. The explanation is one of the two expects to be away hence they can take another on. They are a very honest colored family. I trusted them with my concert grand piano for two years after the house was let to them. There are two egresses in the rear. One to the roof in the rear where a ladder is always there and with a door to open to the roof. Also an entrance to the yard. This was passed on last summer by one of four inspectors and pronounced all right — Nothing more needed.
> — *M. A. Marsh Wellesley.*

Census records of the 1920s suggest otherwise: Sarah Marsh appears to have had ten roomers rather than two, and the inspectors kept after her. She fought back, getting the tenants to write on her behalf. I found a penciled note reading:

"This is to say that I, J. H. Barkly, occupy the house 11 Holy-oke and 3 friend only and have been living here continually since the War. With some number in family (I feel safe) in case of fire as there is no one occupies the top flat. There is a ladder leading to the top." This wooden ladder nailed to the wall at the faucet end of the bathtub was still solidly in place when I moved into my house in 1978.

Later on, Marsh was cited for a faulty chimney that allowed smoke to seep into the house next door. This time she responded with: "I have nothing to do with the repairs at #15 Holyoke Street [#13 had already disappeared] but I do know that the smoke came from there. A man has inspected at 11 H and no repairs are need on the chimney of the property."

In fact, city inspectors had been warning about fire hazards for years. As far back as 1925 they cited seven Holyoke residents for faulty fire escapes, exposed wood lathe near heating units, and deteriorated chimney pipes. These concerns exploded after the catastrophic Coconut Grove tragedy on November 28, 1942, when 492 people either burned to death or were asphyxiated in a fire at the night club located in the present Bay Village on the edge of the South End.

The story of that terrible night and its aftermath is told definitively in Paul Benzaquin's book *Holocaust!*, which chronicles in horrendous detail the origins of the fire, the rapid advance of the flames, how rescue workers labored to remove charred bodies, and how medical staff struggled to treat survivors. The author also tells how volunteers worked to help family members desperately seeking loved ones. As it turned out, the last body to be identified had no recognizable remains except for a door key found in his pants pocket, which police finally traced it to a house on Milford in the South End. Climbing stairs to a second-floor apartment, they found the key belonged to Alexander Dashevsky, a part-time waiter at Coconut Grove.[1]

Soon after I read the Benzaquin book, I ran into Geri Sinclair clipping her hedges in the front yard and asked her if she remembered the night. Geri usually avoids conversations when Holyoke history comes up (she has lived here more than 70 years) but she answered immediately, "Oh, yes, we could see the smoke from the corner of Holyoke and people talked about the fire for weeks afterward. My sister who was living on Holyoke went down the next day to see what she could do. She was a nurse. In fact, she was one of the first black nurses at Boston City Hospital where so many people were taken after the fire."

Other signs of trouble were mounting. I found a study by Walter Firey at Massachusetts Institute of Technology's Rotch Library that said real estate assessment in the South End dropped 34 percent between 1925 and 1940. The percentage of families on public assistance outnumbered every other district in Boston — at one point as high as 46 percent of the district's population. The neighborhood also "led the city in incidence of moral offenses," referring to drunkenness and prostitution.[2]

Threading his way through reams of statistics on the ages of lodgers and their living habits, Firey analyzed the crime

14.

Columbus Avenue, circa 1962.

figures and decided they reflected the lonely lifestyle of South End men. "The lone person, whether he is middle aged and employed or is elderly and retired, will often if not generally have a minimum of furniture and other heavy belongings. Moreover, unless he does considerable entertaining of friends, he has little occasion for a whole house or even for an apartment. A single room will take care of his needs . . . So what do the men do? Play slot machines, buy numbers, meet women, and otherwise "engage in activities that are morally censurable by the scale of values in the larger society." During these mid-century years, the economic underpinnings of the city were cracking, not unlike the brick walls of South End houses. Boston went from ranking as the fourth banking city in the United States to the tenth. Manufacturing dwindled as mills and factories moved elsewhere, and even the fishing industry fell as frozen foods came on the market.[3] Construction was also stagnating. In 1950, only one new building had been completed since 1929.[4]

I found more on the area's declining condition at the Rotch Library in the 1962 *South End Report*, packed with numbers and narrative descriptions and reporting there was a 35 percent reduction in the South End's population between 1950 and 1960.[5] There were 54,000 elderly people in the neighborhood in 1960, 80 percent of whom lived alone, subsisting on incomes of less than $3,000 a year.[6] Other woes included dirty and dangerous streets, crowded living quarters, homes with no yards for outdoor activities, and schools in bad repair. According to a 1960 housing inventory, Bolan said, 11 percent of houses were dilapidated, 44 percent were deteriorating, and 45 percent were unsound. Of the deteriorating units, 59 percent lacked toilets, bathing facilities and hot and cold water for exclusive use of the tenant.[7] Owners were either unable or, in the case of many absentees, unwilling to make needed repairs or reconstruction. "For nearly every environmental standard measurable in statistics, the South End, including Lower Roxbury, ranks the lowest in the metropolitan area."[8]

Almost no one had a chance to observe this better than John Sacco, a Boston policeman who had spent almost all of his 42 years on the force as a South End patrolman and community service officer.[9] When I spoke with Sacco, he recalled the South End of the 1940s and 1950s as a stable community where people got along and where many of the men worked on the railroad, made good money, and wanted their children to go to college. Elderly people in lodging houses who paid their weekly rent from their social security checks were part of neighborhood life. The South End section of the Police Department's District Four had a high concentration of alcoholics but Sacco insisted this wasn't the whole story; the neighborhood was close-knit and felt safe.

It was true that prostitution was a big industry in the South End, but it was also part of the citywide phenomenon and the police simply lived with it. "There were lots of military conventions in the 1950s, and the guys wanted to get drunk and get laid. Everything closed early so hotels put pressure in the courts to wink-wink, blink-blink when the prostitutes got charged or locked up. The court was a revolving door," Sacco said. The women worked for pimps, relying on a system that provided stylish clothes, small luxuries, and spending money to gamble on the dog races. Many prostitutes raised children in respectable style.

However, Sacco agreed with what I had read in studies about the changes at the beginning of the 1960s. Just like the houses, the social fabric began to fray. Drug dealers came into the neighborhood, getting young boys hooked so they would sell to pay for their habit. With women's liberation in the air, Sacco reflected, prostitutes no longer wanted to share a cut with the pimps. Most broke with the men and started working the streets alone. Soon many got involved in drugs, which led them on to more serious crimes. As the golden years came to a close, another change was right around the corner that would reverse some of this — but would also bring change whose merit many South Enders would question for a long time.

Again, it seemed to happen almost overnight.

CHAPTER 7

Another Wave of Newcomers

1960 – 1965

As the 1960s began, the South End was viewed increasingly as unattractive, if not a downright unpleasant place to live. But soon the decade would bring a new generation who saw the district as anything but unappealing. On the contrary, they viewed the neighborhood as a "land of opportunity." John F. Kennedy had just been elected president, and typical of the new generation, these new South Enders welcomed change and adventure.

Geraldine and Tom Ford are African Americans who had met at a Florida college, married, and in the early 1960s, moved to Holyoke Street. Geraldine, a Boston Public Schools teacher, told me that when she and Tom moved in, the

Columbus Avenue blocks from West Newton to Dartmouth were a hodgepodge of aging bow fronts with an abundance of small shops and bars crammed in between. The 411 Club at end of Holyoke was particularly popular — and boisterous! Two gas stations — one at the corner of Holyoke and Columbus and a larger one a few blocks away — contributed to the street's shabby appearance.

The Fords represented the new influx of college-educated young people who bought old houses in the South End with an eye to making them home. They were drawn not only by the reasonable buying prices but by the prospect of living in an interesting and diverse community as well. The press labeled these young people urban pioneers, urban homesteaders, even urban Hippies.

No matter the name, these young people wanted to push boundaries and explore new frontiers. Most could scrape together the down payment for a South End mortgage (in some cases as little as $3,000), and many enjoyed overturning traditional expectations. Their parents and friends told them the South End was dangerous and ugly, but they saw only possibility. Nothing would stop them.

Holyoke Street's Virginia Glennon was typical of the new wave of homesteaders. A graduate of Tufts University and a reviewer and promoter for modern dance groups, Virginia bought #18 Holyoke Street from Mel King, a black leader and activist who would later run for mayor of Boston. Mel wanted to ensure that houses coming onto the market went to people already in the neighborhood so he teamed up with

Keith Bison to do some buying and selective selling. When Virginia learned about his motives, she asked him why he would sell to a white outsider. He replied that he thought she wouldn't break up the house into expensive units. He was right. Virginia bought for $14,000, got a bank loan for $20,000 to make repairs, and kept the building as a two-unit rental for nearly thirty years until her untimely death in 1997.[1]

Another Holyoke homesteader was twenty-two-year-old Joe Linkin who bought his bow front (#28) in 1969. Outraged at rental costs in the city, Joe decided to buy a run-down house that needed fixing, save on expensive repairs, and do the work himself. Mrs. Ethel Holmes, who sold to him for $15,000, said she was fed up with difficult tenants, including one who fell down the stairs, crashed into her, and broke her glasses into her eye. She said she was only too happy to sell. Joe restored, reconfigured, and remodeled his house over time. His basement is stocked with tools, paints, molding pieces, door handles, bathroom fixtures, wood panels, window frames, sinks, and garden planters that he continues to collect, so he always has the requisite materials on hand. In the 1980s Joe installed a large, recycled copper-lined skylight, and he has re-done his own living arrangement and rental units a number of times. At the time of this writing Joe is still at #28, his house, he says, "a work in progress."

Edie and William Schroeder were another story of life on Holyoke in the 1960s. Edie met her future husband while she was at Radcliffe and he was a graduate student in architecture at Harvard. The two married in 1964 and, with fellow student

John Bassett, bought #33 Holyoke for $7,500. Though still living in Cambridge they hoped to some day restore the fine features of the original house while being decent landlords in the interim. Bassett agreed to do the fixing up while Bill Schroeder said he would take care of the paperwork. It turned out that neither had much appetite for the job. Bassett, in particular, disapproved of the "gentrification" taking place in the neighborhood, resisting good management practices, failing to collect rents from recalcitrant tenants, and refusing to evict them as income dwindled.

Meanwhile, Bill and Edie moved to Rutland Square and after having two children, decided to use the basement of #33 Holyoke for a school. Inspired by A. S. Neill's *Summerhill: A Radical Approach to Rearing Children* and John Holt's *How Children Fail*, the Schroeder's and their friends created a nongraded, active-learning school for seven to eight children. Without getting licensed, the group advertised for students and hired a young teacher who subscribed to their educational philosophy. The teacher worked four days a week and on the fifth day, parents took the students, who ranged in age from five to twelve, to visit a factory, museum, sewage treatment plant, zoo, or any other site with educational value.

The founders of the Rowhouse School, as the Holyoke venture was called, began to have problems when the mother of a black child insisted that the adults in charge needed to exert greater control over the children. Other clashes surfaced and after a year the school closed. Bassett sold to another partner while the Schroeders were in the process of getting a

15.

Class in a South End school on Groton Street, 1962.

divorce. Eventually Bill Schroeder sold #33 to tenants, offering to take the mortgage himself. The effort was typical of the times, and though it didn't last, it was cheerfully abandoned for other ventures. Edie became active in a food coop, but that comes later.

Early homesteaders were, for the most part, people who valued the racial and ethnic mix of the South End. Even though they had purchased houses from aging residents, they were worried about dislocating people who had been in the neighborhood a long time. Caught up in the idealism and optimism of the 1960s, they tried both to fit into the neighborhood, and to change it. Edie Schroeder said she was attracted to the South End almost solely for its openness to racial and economic diversity. Raised in the debutante society of Baltimore, Edie wanted her own children to experience more than a "lily white" America.

Having moved to Boston for graduate school at Massachusetts Institute of Technology, Ken Kruckemeyer found the South End almost by chance while helping a friend deliver birch timber to a house on West Brookline Street. Soon after, Ken and his wife, Ann, bought #12 Holyoke. Duncan Bolt, from a West Canton family living one street over, remembers Ken helping teenagers from the Tubman House turn the vacant, junk-filled railroad area at the end of Holyoke into a stage where kids could put on music shows in the summer. Ken was typical of the new residents who saw the South End as an good place to build community across race and backgrounds, Duncan said.

Many of these newcomers came to the South End with an interest in social work or community organizing. Decades after Robert Woods lived there, Carolyn Ann Boehne moved into #20 Union Park after college. She met her future husband Gene there, and both were active in community affairs — Carolyn Ann in food co-ops, the League of Women Voters, and teenage groups at Cathedral housing, and Gene at the Shawmut Neighborhood Center and the Tubman House on Holyoke. Later Carolyn Ann worked in Head Start and Gene eventually became a community organizer for seventeen different organizations throughout the South End, helping low-income individuals hold on to their homes and take advantage of federal, state, and local programs that were becoming available at the time. Gene said he and other organizers worked to encourage struggling individuals and families to improve their lives by working together. Gene recalls that Bill Russell, the legendary Celtics basketball player, lived in the neighborhood in those days and often came by to lend a hand.

Of course, all this new energy drew real estate buyers who could easily imagine property values increasing with all the improvements. This meant older homeowners were being offered seemingly astronomical amounts of money for homes they were hard pressed to keep, especially with rising tax rates and burdensome repair costs. The Boston Redevelopment Authority is a warren of little rooms on the ninth floor of City Hall. Thumbing through dozens of South End population and housing studies stored in file boxes there, I culled the following facts documenting conditions at the time. For example, the median income of South Enders was $4,542 in 1960; it would increase by 74 percent by the end of the decade and more than double by 1978;[2] the assessed values of the South End increased by 28 percent in the eight years following 1965;[3] in the two years of 1970–72 alone, taxes increased by 19 percent.[4]

After Harold Hill left for college and the army, he moved back to live briefly at Katherine Robinson's house on Braddock Park. Harold said he would always remember the day when he was on Holyoke with friends. Two white men approached one of the older black homeowners sweeping his walk and offered him $22,000 for his house. "That was #5 Holyoke,

I remember, and it was the first one on the block to go down," Harold said, meaning it was the first sold to a developer. Ena Harris of Braddock Park complained that one realtor dogged her for more than a year, telephoning her, stopping by on the street, trying to catch her doing errands. He kept pressuring her to sell until one day she told him in no uncertain terms never to bother her again.

One new project offered hope to long-term South Enders threatened with losing their homes in a housing market that was heating up at a rapid pace. Boston planners and politicians, like those in cities around the country, had been seeking to develop low-cost public housing for returning war veterans and their growing families after World War II. The deteriorating old bow fronts and hotels along Columbus Avenue presented just the kind of site needed to construct new apartment units. Federal funding for such "replacement housing" through a House and Urban Development (HUD) program called Demonstration Disposition enabled local nonprofits to get into the housing development business. The Union United Methodist Church at the corner of West Newton and Columbus was in an excellent position to take advantage of this opportunity.

The church itself, a striking Victorian Gothic structure made of Roxbury puddingstone and incorporating a 420-foot steeple and sanctuary lined with richly colored stained glass windows, was originally owned and occupied by Congregationalists. The building was purchased by the former Bromfield Street Methodist Church that moved from Beacon Hill in 1948. In 1964 a young Boston University–educated

16.

Methunion buildings on Columbus Avenue.

minister, Reverend Gil Caldwell, took the helm. Caldwell, who had taken part in the Student Nonviolent Coordinating Committee's (SNCC) voter registration drive in Mississippi, saw his new position at Union Methodist as a platform for addressing racism in Boston — and for making the Union United Methodist a low-income housing developer for South End blacks. The project, begun in the early 1960s, took a long time to be completed, but when it was, there were four large flat-front apartment buildings along Columbus Avenue at the corners of Braddock, Holyoke and West Canton Streets. Union United Methodist Church held the deed and was in charge of management. Altogether the project would provide 140 new units of housing. It was a true, albeit hard won, South End success story.

Urban Renewal

1965 – 1975

Boston's urban renewal hit the city like a tidal wave but it's hard to pinpoint exactly when it began. Did it start when the "rascal king" Mayor James Michael Curley went to the penitentiary for eighteen months and a City Hall clerk by the name of John Hynes temporarily took over — later becoming the mayor responsible for putting in the new Central Artery to bolster downtown business?[1] Or did it begin when the city displaced approximately 7,000 immigrants in the West End to build high-rise apartments in the place of the existing tenements?[2] Or was the first big event of urban renewal in the 1950s when wrecking balls slammed through the low-income housing in the South End's New York Streets — an eighteen-acre community of Irish, West Indians, Portuguese, Albanians, Greeks, Armenians, Jews, Filipinos, Chinese, Syrians, and Lebanese whose homes got cleared for an industrial area?[3] All these were clearly predecessors, but the full impact of urban renewal on the South End was felt most profoundly in the 1960s.

It was the Housing and Urban Development (HUD) Act of 1949 that set Boston's urban renewal into motion. Designed to rebuild deteriorated sections of U. S. cities, the act called for public authorities to administer programs that would revitalize their own cities. Boston designated its Planning Board (first created in 1913) to be in charge. Because HUD required a plan for the whole community, however, the Board had to come up with a general plan. It developed one in 1950 that called for slum clearance and redevelopment of 20 percent of the city (2,700 acres) over a twenty-five-year period — a plan primarily designed to encourage the transformation of downtown Boston into a business center for the whole metropolitan area. After the general plan was finished, the city created the Boston Redevelopment Authority (BRA) in 1957 to focus specifically on finances and action steps to implement the plan.[4]

When John Collins became Boston's mayor in 1960, one of his first actions was to appoint an urban planner, Edward Logue, to head the BRA. Logue, a Yale-educated lawyer with a reputation for being pugnacious, did not hesitate to plunge in immediately to implement his own vision for the city. Armed by Mayor Collins with broad, centralized power, Logue began to transform the face of Boston in ways that would make it almost unrecognizable twenty years later.

Logue's first target was the Prudential Center — twenty-eight acres of Boston and Albany Railroad land that Mayor John Hynes, years before, had dreamed of developing into a fifty-two-floor office building with two adjacent apartment buildings. Financing had reached a stalemate due to disputes between government and community over how to pay for it and the project had stalled. With Boston's 1959 tax base 25 percent smaller than it had been twenty years earlier, opposing groups fought to make the project financially feasible without incurring massive expense.[5] Eventually opposing parties went all the way to the Massachusetts Supreme Judicial Court in an effort to settle the conflict. The case was in court when Logue came on board, and it wasn't long before he proposed a solution to the Prudential logjam. He argued that if the city described the old railroad bed as a *blighted area* needing renewal, it could receive HUD funding that would be preferable to any finance package presented so far. Persuading leaders to agree, Logue, the mayor, and several well-connected individuals went down to Washington to personally make their case to HUD. In a matter of weeks, Boston received notice that federal financing would be forthcoming. The Supreme Judicial Court decided the dispute in favor of the city and gave approval for a $200 million bond issue tying together a Massachusetts Turnpike extension, a 2,500-car parking garage, and the high-rise office and apartment buildings. It would turn the Prudential project into a "renewal" reality[6] and in six years the Prudential Center was completed.

Having the Prudential Towers next door to the South End gave the neighborhood its first glimpse of the high-impact development to come. Instead of the old railroad bed, Holyokers and neighbors now had a shopping center rivaling downtown's right at the neighborhood's borders.[7] Maybe the most significant fact for South Enders was Star Market, a new supermarket — almost the only one in all of in-town Boston. When my children, Sam and Emmy, were young, we walked to the market, carriage in tow, to make shopping an evening's excursion there. The mix of shoppers from Back Bay and the South End was colorful, and activity in the aisles always varied. People snapped and quarreled at the supermarket, muttered to themselves, or simply ambled the aisles without ever purchasing. Movie and theater celebrities residing in the Tower apartments slipped down to shop in sports-clothes disguises.

Once Collins and Logue had solved the Prudential project, they looked to other parts of the city that might be ripe for renewal. The first to be targeted was Boston's downtown Scollay Square district (an area of sixty acres that included twenty-two streets), which was leveled and replaced by a vast new Government Center. This project was completed in 1968.[8] Next came the West End, bordering Storrow Drive and the backside of Beacon Hill. The West End had been demolished by the time I returned to Boston a decade later, but I would remember it as others would by a huge billboard along Storrow Drive that read: "If you lived here, you'd be home by now" — a cheery enough statement, but hardly revealing the devastation that had occurred.

The saga of the West End is best chronicled in Herbert Gans's classic account, *The Urban Villagers*, which I read sitting in the park outside the South End library branch one summer afternoon in 1998. Gans had moved to the West End, renting an apartment for forty-six dollars a month, in order to observe and converse with individuals and families (mostly Italian and Jewish immigrants) during the urban renewal years of 1958–60. Contrary to what city planners thought, Gans reported, the West End was a healthy neighborhood with a robust community, a strong sense of itself, and a determination to collectively care for its members. When renewal leveled all of its homes and services, residents were scattered from one end of the city to the other, the entire community destroyed as the New York Streets had been in the decade before.

Once the West End renewal was completed Logue and his team turned to neighborhoods further out. Roxbury's Washington Park (with 25 percent of the area targeted to be "cleared" and the rest upgraded) was the first, then Charlestown (where residents lost 11 percent of existing housing), then Allston-Brighton.[9] The South End would be next.

When South Enders saw what urban renewal meant to the West End and other neighborhoods, they were wary to say the least. Fortifying themselves by organizing into small neighborhood and community groups (at one time as many as 155 different organizations), residents began challenging the BRA's plans with visions of their own. Logue, working to garner support from select groups, pushed for a new prosperous middle-class district, but grassroots groups fought back in favor of a plan responsive to present residents and their collective wishes. Finally, after hundreds of meetings, both sides came together over a plan in 1965 that more or less divided the area into residential and industrial zones, or "ovals," as they were called. The plan called for over 3,000 new private rental units, 300 new public housing units on scattered sites, 500 new housing units for the elderly, plus new schools, playgrounds and parks, making it the largest federal government-approved urban renewal project in the United States. The approved plan may have come too late, however. A new sentiment for change driven by "the people" as opposed to the experts was sweeping the country, and South End renewal-plan skeptics were not going to drop their vigilance, especially in relation to housing.[10]

Mel King (by the 1960s a resident of Yarmouth, two streets over from Holyoke) and others distrusted BRA promises to relocate those who would be displaced. Gathering a group called the Community Assembly for a United South End (CAUSE) that focused on tenant needs, committee members undertook a block-by-block organizing effort in 1966–68 to warn residents that the BRA planned to take their houses. In the immediate Holyoke neighborhood that meant four long swatches of housing on Columbus Avenue — and scores of homes on Yarmouth and Dartmouth Streets.[11]

By this time (1968) the houses of a hundred families along

17.

West Canton Street, next to Holyoke, circa 1962.

the existing railroad tracks had already been demolished, with tenants receiving no alternative housing.[12] The emptied land was blacktopped to serve as a parking lot while the city considered options for the eventual development of Copley Place. One April morning CAUSE began distributing leaflets on cars coming into the lot to say that it was banning parking in protest. Several people were arrested before the day was out, but CAUSE members continued to protest, setting up barbeque grills, eating and sleeping on the land for three days.

The demonstration drew onlookers by the thousands — and national publicity.

Mel King went on to become the Director of Boston's new Urban League and founder of the New Majority as well as an author and teacher — but what happened on that parking lot became legend. Over the next twenty years, a core group of tireless South Enders, led by Mel and Ken Kruckemeyer, battled for housing on that parking lot, meeting hundreds of times to shape a vision for mixed-income housing on the site. Convening most of the time in living rooms, the group hammered out a plan calling for 25 percent low-income housing, 50 percent moderate, and 25 percent market rate. The structure that the group (called the Tent City Task Force) finally managed to get built was a large five-level apartment complex occupying almost the entire Dartmouth Street block bounded by Columbus and the Southwest Corridor Park. It was ready for its first residents in 1988.[13]

I moved to Hanover, New Hampshire, with my new husband in the fall of 1965 so I missed much of South End life for the next decade. But the Dwyers remained in Boston, in the thick of the urban-renewal storm. I later learned from the Dwyers and others what happened around St. Stephen's during those years. As the wreckers and dumpsters came in for clearing the thirty acres of old houses in this area (Parcel 19), Bill Dwyer and others decided, like Mel King in the Dartmouth Street area, they wouldn't take a chance the government would deliver on its promise to relocate displaced individuals and families. With money from a local foundation, Bill's group hired community organizer Carmelo Iglesias to create an Emergency Tenants Council (ETC) as a watchdog group to monitor BRA relocation activities. ETC eventually became Inquilinos Boricuas en Accion (IBA), the tenant-controlled organization that developed Parcel 19 into Villa Victoria. Again, it took endless meetings and tireless wrangling, but by the end of the decade ETC had created a nationally recognized development of mixed housing units and a range of shops and community services.[14] And the community had done it!

Meanwhile Holyoke Street and neighboring streets were losing houses to a transportation project related to housing issues as well. This project began back in 1948, when the Massachusetts Department of Public Works issued a Master Highway Plan calling for two beltways and an extension of I-95 (coming from Providence) to go from Route 128 into Hyde Park and then Boston. The outer Route 128 beltway already existed but a new inner beltway was designed to loop through Brookline and Boston, cross the Charles River, and run through Cambridge's Central Square until it reached I-93 in Somerville. The plan again was supposed to make travel easier for commuting suburbanites, who would hopefully keep the downtown alive.

Demolition for the new I-95 extension began in the mid 1960s, but here too, the plan met a groundswell of resistance. People all the way from Roslindale and Hyde Park to Somerville opposed it. Calling themselves the Greater Boston Committee on the Transportation Crisis (GBCTC), a group led a "People Before Highways Day" campaign, convening events

18.

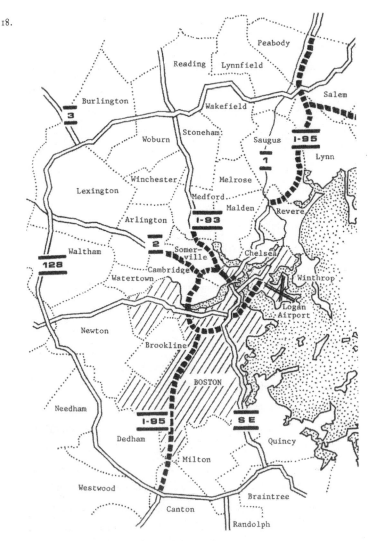

Graphic rendition of the 1960s highway plan.

Swath of land that South Enders stopped from becoming a highway.

and demonstrations to stop the highways from tearing up neighborhoods. Ann Hershfang, Ken Kruckemeyer, Barry Adams, and David Scott spearheaded the fight in the South End with others joining in.

Eventually Governor Francis Sargent and Mayor Kevin White conceded that the I-95 extension and the new inner belt were not good ideas, announcing in November 1972 that the project would be dropped. A segment of the inner belt had been completed (present Melnia Cass Boulevard) but the I-95 extension would never be constructed. The land that had been cleared for it would be used for a relocated Orange Line track to run parallel with existing rail lines. Later, after scores of meetings over a period of years, that swath would become a public park. That story comes in Chapter 11.

Once the dust had settled, South Enders who had fought to halt the highway project began looking at streets and traffic problems closer to home. The South End Committee on Transportation, led by Ann Hershfang, Ellen Gordon, and Ken Kruckemeyer, along with others who came on board, undertook a study of transportation and pedestrian problems in the South End. The introduction to the Committee's proposal reads:

> Transportation problems affect all residents of the South End. The cars of the commuters daily clog our streets, threatening our safety and adding noise, dirt and pollution to our urban environment. Trucks continually shake our houses as they cross from one side of the city to another. Parking for those automobiles becomes increasingly difficult as they vie with commuters for space and are subject to discriminatory enforcement of existing parking regulations. . . . The benefits [of this proposed plan] should also go beyond transportation to spin-offs such as housing rehabilitation, park construction and local retail development.[15]

Which is, indeed, what happened.

The committee presented the plan to the South End Project Area Committee (SEPAC), the elected group designated by the city to work with the BRA on urban renewal) gained the organization's approval, and eventually the city's approval as well. In the end, the group managed to save both Columbus and Tremont from becoming main arteries into the city by narrowing Columbus from four lanes to two and preventing a widening of Tremont. Over time, these persistent South Enders changed traffic directions on streets, diminished through traffic, widened sidewalks, influenced parking regulations, increased available green space, initiated street landscaping, and more. Many believe their work saved the character and pleasant ambiance of the South End that has lasted to this day.

More Dissent

1975 – 1980

One evening in the late 1970s I stopped to talk to a group of older men (mostly in their seventies and eighties) sitting on a makeshift bench outside of Charlie's Sandwich Shoppe. The bench and the silver-painted electric control box on Braddock Park across from the drug store were popular summer gathering places for African American and West Indian "old timers." Occasionally the men would recognize and nod to newcomers like me, but mostly they kept to themselves. I knew many of them had been born in the South End and hung around the neighborhood in the daytime, but wanted to know how many still lived in the South End. Punching each other on the shoulders and laughing as

I waited for an answer, one said, "We all born here and we all gonna die here. Nobody gonna push us out."

The comment reflected growing tensions in the South End around displacement. While the early battles to halt the demolition of South End housing were drawing to a close, the struggle to keep the housing affordable for long time residents was not. Hundreds of houses were coming on the market. Federal low-interest loans were available for homeowners wanting to do their own repairs, but many of the older residents were either tenants, or didn't qualify for loans. The men I talked to in front of Charlie's that night had seen the housing go to outsiders. Their shoulder punching was no joke.

Mayor Kevin White took office in 1970 immediately announcing he would help clean up the the South End, partially by having the BRA purchase aging properties from owners willing to sell. Many houses now belonged to the children of elderly or deceased South Enders, and these young people did not want the headaches of being landlords or property owners. They were only too happy to sell. According to Boston Police Officer John Sacco, what happened was more sinister than Mayor White's plan appeared. More often than not, the BRA would get a straw man to buy up the house for virtually nothing and then sell it to a developer. Some of these straw men, Sacco said, "did very well." He knew of one retired insider who had a lot of mysterious cash and a questionably high pension — even a pension for his cat. This rapid turnover to developers was one factor contributing to rising housing costs. Another was the desire of developers and new homeowners to increase values by preserving the neighborhood's historic character.

I learned almost immediately about the arguments over historic preservation and its potential to displace residents soon after I moved back to the South End in 1976. One group, calling themselves the Committee of Citizens for a Balanced South End, hoped to increase property values in the neighborhood by emphasizing its aesthetic and historic appeal. This group, arguing that the South End had more than its share of run-down, subsidized, or otherwise unattractive properties, did not want it to have more. Another group, many of them white homeowners who bought in the early- to mid-1960s, argued that displacing people who had lived in the neighborhood for generations was unacceptable. Those in the latter group valued the diversity of the neighborhood, and resisted the prospect of an all-white, middle- and upper-class community. At one point the Committee of Citizens sued to stop further low-income development. Advocates for the housing-disenfranchised, fighting just as hard, continued to exert pressure on the BRA with the same fervor others had given to Tent City. Much of the tension seemed to come out of varying opinions about the South End Historical Society (SEHS).

SEHS had been incorporated in 1967, and while many of its members were concerned about people losing their housing, the society itself became known as a group mainly concerned with South End architecture. As residents became increasingly polarized around the issue of "preservation," the society became a target of demonstrations, particularly during their gala fundraising balls launched in the early 1970s. At one such event advocates for low-income housing staged a protest that included a sign reading "South End Historical Society is an Upper Class KKK."

In fairness it must be said the roots for SEHS go deep and many feel indebted to the organization for doing much to save the neighborhood's beauty. The desire to preserve valued buildings had been growing in the United States for a long time, becoming formalized in 1966 when the government passed the National Preservation Act to protect valued historic properties throughout the country. Soon after, SEHS members and other area residents applied to have the South End's 300 acres of Victorian housing (the largest in the country) listed on the National Register of Historic Places. They succeeded in their efforts in 1973.

Meanwhile the Commonwealth of Massachusetts was crafting its own preservation legislation, including regulations that would prove to have considerable impact on everyday life in the South End. An act of 1975 created the Boston Landmarks Commission, and before long South Enders and various consultants produced a study proposing the establishment of a South End Landmark District Commission. This application was approved in 1983. Since then the Commission has set policy and issued strict regulations for what could and could not be done to the exterior appearance of properties. A twelve-panel, fine-print brochure outlines the categories regulated by the commission: steps and stairs, railing

20.

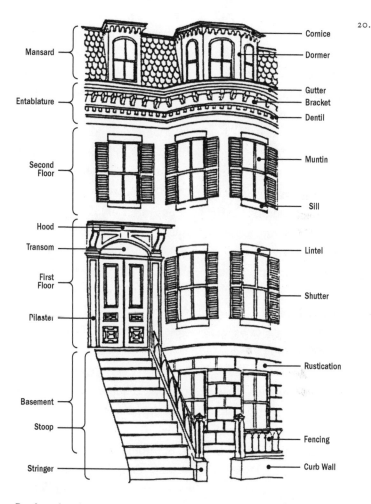

Mansard

Entablature

Second
Floor

Hood

Transom

First
Floor

Pilaster

Basement

Stoop

Stringer

Cornice

Dormer

Gutter

Bracket

Dentil

Muntin

Sill

Lintel

Shutter

Rustication

Fencing

Curb Wall

Brochure drawing.

balustrades and balconies, entryways, exterior walls, window openings and replacements, bays and oriels, roofs, fences, fire escapes, and more. Two of the panels contained a house sketch with labels for all the typical South End house details: cornice, dormer, mansard, dentil, muntin, lintel, and others. Over the years the South End Commission's influence on community life has grown, thanks to its authority to rule on disputes between homeowners and developers seeking waivers and special consideration.

The Buildings Department and the Zoning Commission were drawn into the fray as well. On Holyoke Street, a developer was extending the back of Chris Visitinsky's neighbor at #38 to make larger apartments when she rallied neighbors to fight with her to halt the expansion. Not only did she succeed in convincing the court that the zoning should be changed, but that it would be applied retroactively. The developer was forced to bring the rear of the building back in line with those on the rest of the block. A similar case occurred at #7 Holyoke but this time the developer was able to slip through the regulations with a series of ownership maneuvers. As a result, the building has a large extension that cuts off sunlight and disrupts the original line of houses from Columbus to Southwest Corridor Park. I have always lamented that I did not fight that change myself as it drastically cuts off sunlight during the summer months.

Another Holyoke house failed to get regulation attention in time. Louis Silipo purchased #5 with a plan to make it into apartments. This location had often been reported to the

Buildings Department by neighbors concerned that the wall facing the alley was more than vulnerable; it was downright shaky. As workmen removed big sections of bricks, they created an enormous hole in the side of the building that several people predicted would cause the wall to crumble. Mothers in the adjacent Methunion building threatened to take Silipo to court, but they didn't move quickly enough. One night in the wee hours, the wall buckled and large sections collapsed. I discovered later that kind of episode was not uncommon. A house at the end of Braddock Park came down in the early 1960s — on this occasion when people were sleeping upstairs. The story circulated that when the wall fell, it pulled the floors down at an angle that caused people to roll out of their beds and almost out of the building.

Battles over South End housing renewal and transportation plans weren't the only confrontations occurring as the 1970s began. An equally dramatic one affecting the entire city surfaced around this same time. Its story officially began in 1971 when the Massachusetts Board of Education told the Boston School Committee it must comply with the state Racial Imbalance Act of 1965. When the School Committee refused to do so, the state ordered a $200 million freeze on new school construction, threatening to withdraw $14 million in state aid for non-compliance as well. In response, the Boston School Committee brought suit against the state board. At this point the Boston branch of the National Association for the Advancement of Colored People (NAACP) turned its own plaintiff-based case into a class action suit against the School

Committee. Finally, in 1974, U.S. District Judge W. Arthur Garrity delivered his now legendary 152-page decision declaring the entire school system to be unconstitutionally segregated, a decision unanimously upheld by the U.S. Court of Appeals. The city was forced to desegregate sixty-one of Boston's eighty public schools by the first day of classes in 1974. The decision meant 17,000 children would be transported out of their neighborhoods on buses.[1]

Many saw busing as a desperately needed measure to break down prejudice in the city's ethnically homogenous neighborhoods; others viewed it as destructive because it took children out of neighborhood schools. Regardless, it held hardship for families on either side of the argument.

In his book *Common Ground* (1985), J. Anthony Lukas chronicles the lives of three families during Boston's busing crisis. Two of the families were from the South End: one was an African American family by the name of Twymon, early tenants of a four-bedroom unit in the Methunion building on Columbus at the corner of Holyoke Street; the second was the Divers, a white couple who had a house on West Newton in 1970. In his exhaustive history of racial conflict as it shattered individual lives and communities, Lukas tells how both families were deeply affected by the conflict. Swept up in the rage and chaos of the time, the Twymon children became both victims and perpetrators of crime and human tragedy. The Divers, both from privileged backgrounds (Colin Diver was a graduate of Harvard Law School), struggled to hold on to ideals of equal opportunity. In their case street crime, growing out of festering resentments among blacks as the number of affluent white people in the neighborhood grew, finally overwhelmed them and they moved out.[2]

Court-ordered busing became a big obstacle for South End families involved in developing the Bancroft School — a grass-roots project emerging out of parent efforts to improve public schools in the neighborhood during the 1960s. Mothers and fathers, getting permission to use space in the vacated Bancroft on Warren Avenue, hoped that un-graded classrooms, innova-tive teaching methods, and close parental involvement (such as teaching occasional classes themselves) would improve the quality of education their children received. Soon they added

21.

Old Bancroft and Rice Schools on Appleton Street, circa 1960.

grades and opened classrooms in the Rice School next door. The initiative became a rallying point for South Enders eager to improve schools and make the community a desirable place to raise their children.

The Bancroft project was important for another reason. It was a fully integrated program, bringing students from Hispanic, Chinese, and African American families of the South End together with the new white homesteaders. In some respects it was an ideal project, carrying out exactly what the "forced busing" agenda was attempting to accomplish. But when the needed funding did not come through, and the School Department dragged its heels on essential building improvements, the venture came to close. It had lasted 12 years and been a powerful experience for the families involved, but times had changed, especially in the city's education system.[3]

I enrolled my son Sam as a first grader at the Blackstone School when we moved to Boston from Vermont in 1976. The school, built of a new design with large spaces for "open classrooms," was a concession to Bancroft parents and others pressuring the school department to adopt more interesting environments and more enlightened pedagogy to educate children. The Blackstone, however, had a number of organizational problems and I eventually asked for Sam's transfer to Roxbury's Trotter School, a magnet school that parents often chose because the facilities were better and teachers deemed more skilled. My daughter Emily entered the Trotter as a kindergartner in 1979. By then families were getting used to both the benefits and difficulties of busing children and most people, even Bancroft parents, went along with the city-wide desegregation plan.

In spite of the struggles and battles occurring during these years, South Enders tried to carry on life as usual. City children and teens didn't have large grassy vacant lots and traffic-free streets for after-school games and play, but they found their own amusements as children always do. Duncan Bolt said that when he was growing up the boys played stickball and football in the street. Max Moore whose architect father bought a Holyoke house in 1971 when Max was ten said he remembers playing a tag game where "it" stood in the middle of the street while others ran back and forth between parked cars to the "safety zone" on the stoop. My son Sam remembers shooting baskets with Yoyo Dwyer in the improvised basketball courts at the end of Holyoke and riding bikes.

Emily was almost four when we moved to Holyoke. She remembers jump rope games, tying one end of the rope to a parked car handle when short of playmates. She also played Mother-May-I and hopscotch — albeit on long stretches of broken sidewalk. I remember her playing dentist with Alissa Ocassio, using a goose-necked office lamp, hand mirror, magnifying glass, geometry compass, and a hair dryer for equipment.

South End churches continued to be places for people to gather and socialize — the ones near Holyoke being Union United Methodist on Columbus, and Concord Baptist on Warren Avenue. Both had large congregations, numerous choirs, clubs, and a long list of activities and special events for members. On Sundays and holidays, cars lined Appleton Street and the Columbus Avenue median so families could attend these churches. Church secretary Mozel Kyle told me Concord Baptist was built in 1868 but didn't become a largely black congregation until 1916. Since then, it has grown to have 1100 members. Most (at least 60 percent) come from Boston neighborhoods, Kyle said, including Roxbury, Dorchester, and Mattapan, sometimes miles away.[4]

A newer institution bringing people together was the neighborhood food co-op. I joined the one at Bill Satterthwaite's on Claremont Street. Every Thursday, those of us in the group would meet in Bill's living room to count out or weigh portions ordered the previous week. Our children would run around in the basement or outdoors while the adults swapped recipes and talked about the quality of produce that week. Co-ops lasted through the 1970s and into the early 1980s, but by then the South End population had become more prosperous and this "economy" finally fell out of fashion. The phenomenon was taken up by a young couple who opened a store selling health foods and wooden toys in Brookline. It was called Bread and Circus and grew to include five stores in other locations before it was purchased by a conglomerate Whole Foods Market in 1992. The rest, as they say, is history.

The 1970s drew to a close with a brief interlude children and adults alike will never forget — the blizzard of 1978. For thirty-two hours, beginning on February 6, snow fell ceaselessly until it had reached a record twenty-seven inches of

22.

Sam and Emmy Potts in Titus Sparrow Park during the 1978 blizzard.

accumulation, drifting in places up to fifteen feet. Schools closed, streets became impassable, stores ran out of goods, and a profound quiet settled over the city. Once the storm passed, however, everyone began digging out of their houses and into the drifted streets. Some people put on their skies and made trails; others found slopes to sled. Still others made igloos and ice caves in avalanches. I had a friend in the Back Bay who wanted to bring her two children over to play with mine. We couldn't imagine how they would get through the snow to visit until we looked out the window an hour later. Judy was arriving with her two children on a toboggan drawn by their dog, a husky.

Altogether it had been a rugged decade, but the neighborhood managed to hold together, even rally as it had after the blizzard. The next decade would bring less contention, but it would not stop the momentum of change.

Housing Multiplied

1980 – 1990

The *South End News*, a small twenty-four-page newspaper with local stories, features, and reviews, had its first edition February 15, 1980. Begun by Alison Barnet and Skip Rosenthal with a loan from Skip's father, the two had the copy typeset, but laid out the paper themselves, using a roller and paste. Once the paper was printed in a Revere shop, Skip would load bundles and drop them at various restaurants, liquor, and drug stores in the neighborhood. The paper was free.

Although fairly new to the South End, I was excited to hear about a local newspaper; one fall evening that year I called Alison and offered to write for it if she needed something covered. Over the next few years I wrote dozens of stories

— many of them on housing issues: tenants' battles to keep their apartments in the old Chickering Piano Factory; Methunion residents' fight against auction of their buildings; and efforts to make the Frankie O'Day block on Columbus into a co-op. Later I wrote about threats to close the South End branch of the Boston Public Library; struggles to get more community gardening spaces; neighborhood shops (hardware, barber, and corner markets); and finally some columns on interesting South End individuals.

The front page of that first *South End News* described what was happening on Holyoke Street and elsewhere, leading with the headline "Court to Rule on Condo Eviction," followed by an article about the attempted eviction of Viviana Munoz and her three children from her apartment at #22 Dartmouth Street — a building that was sold twice on the same day as prices soared. Other headlines were: "BRA Deadline Nears," "Digital Opens Local Facility," and "City Funds Blackstone Renovation." The stories foretold the rapid turnover of properties on block after block in the neighborhood.

By the 1980s the trickle of newcomers to the area had become a veritable river. After all, South Enders could walk to the Boston Public Library, Symphony Hall, Jordan Hall, the Museum of Fine Arts, Fenway Park, and Newbury Street. The Boston Center for the Arts (on Tremont Street) with its exhibit hall, art gallery, and small theaters was close to almost everyone who lived in the neighborhood. Prudential Center's shopping mall with its dozens of shops, restaurants, kiosks, and vast food emporium could compete, maybe even outshine, downtown as the city's center of commercial gravity.

The convenience and ambiance of the South End was causing an explosion in condo conversions. Between the years 1969–85 a total of 1,367 had been built.[1] All of a sudden entrepreneurs were snatching up buildings and turning them into privately-owned units with a mind to attract young buyers wanting an urban life style. Although the city passed an ordinance in 1983 to protect tenants threatened with conviction by developers pressuring owners to sell, conversion progressed at an alarming pace. Mark Goldweitz bought several houses on West Canton, one street over from Holyoke, moving quickly to close deals. Using the same cookie-cutter design (exposed brick, new oak flooring, skylights, roof decks, and back porches) for houses he acquired and converted to apartments, Goldweitz seemed to transform the block in a few short years.

Those of us on Holyoke Street watched with alarm as condo fever took hold. Dumpsters appeared on the street daily, with enormous gray chutes jerry-rigged from connected garbage cans coming from windows on upper floors to bring slabs of old plaster, woodwork, doors, flooring, bathtubs, toilets, and abandoned furnishings to dumpsters below. A huge bin would fill in a few days, get hauled away, and a new one appear immediately in its place. A host of panel trucks (plumbers, electricians, carpenters, and floor sanders) lined the curbs or double-parked in the alley. Weekdays began to the sound of cracking studs and buzzing table saws as early as 5:00 A.M.

Six houses on Holyoke Street provide a representative sampling of what was happening:

23.

New construction on Holyoke Street, 1997.

#5 HOLYOKE STREET. This building was owned by a woman on West Canton Street who used it, according to a number of long-time residents, as a house of prostitution for decades. Louis Silipo lived a few blocks over on Pembroke Street and bought the house in 1980 with the intention of making it into four luxury condo apartments. He ran into a number of construction problems, including the precarious outer wall along the alley discussed in the previous chapter, but eventually did manage to develop the property, selling off the units one by one. Two were bought by Eunice Harps, a woman who worked in the banking industry and later in a local nonprofit; she eventually purchased a third as well.

#7 HOLYOKE STREET. After college, Michael Lerner worked in a community development agency. He and his wife Jennifer, a librarian at the *Boston Globe*, had bought this former rooming house in the 1970s. They had remodeled much of the house and put in a new apartment on the top floor, but after their second child was born, the couple decided to sell and move where they would have more outdoor space. The new owner hired a developer and obtained a permit to build out into backyard. The house became five two-bedroom condominiums — the largest building on the block. It all happened so quickly while ownership seemed to shift between owner and developer that none of us protested the addition. The developer who ended up with the ownership had no trouble selling the units and at least one tenant, Nina Garfinkle, has stayed. Other owners have come and gone, most living in the house for relatively short periods of time.

#9 HOLYOKE STREET. This house stayed in the hands of the Holder family who managed it as a boarding house from the 1920s into the 1980s. The Holders' son Clarence, whose daughter lived in the house for a while, eventually rented to two neighborhood people, one a kindly older black man everyone knew as Gus, and the other a younger somewhat mysterious tenant who had an assortment of visitors arriving at the house in elegant cars, even limos, at odd hours of the night. The building gradually fell into disrepair and Clarence, living outside Boston, decided to sell.

A Texas contractor bought the house in 1988 and began construction to convert it into four condominiums, intending to live in the first one with his new bride from Texas. Unfamiliar with the quirks and problems that come with a 120-year-old house, however, the new owner made ill-advised changes like re-routing drainpipes and venting dryers in awkward places. His new bride came, and deliveries for furnishings and kitchenware mounted, but the project seemed to have lost its luster and the couple left after two years. Some of the Texan's construction decisions continued to dog tenants for years to come.

#15 HOLYOKE STREET. This was another longtime rooming house, owned by the Weymans until a schoolteacher, Barbara Burman, bought the building in the 1970s. Barbara added a kitchen on the fourth floor and made that and the top floor into a duplex where she lived while renting out the lower floors. In 1987 she sold to an inexperienced developer who created a third apartment (on the basement level), intending to rent all three units until condo prices went even higher. Neighbors and tenants complained the developer neglected the property, ignoring leaks and drafty windows, and angering property managers hired to respond to complaints. Finally the owner hired builders to create legal condominiums, but then failed to supply funds for them to do the job properly. New owners came and went, constantly frustrated by construction mistakes and corner-cutting workmanship that hailed back to the year of Barbara Burman's sale. The building is still constantly undergoing changes.

#24 HOLYOKE STREET. In the 1980s Mrs. Hill was still living in #24 and still keeping renters but she faced a dilemma: she didn't want to manage the house any longer, but she didn't want to move out of the house and the neighborhood. Her solution was to find a buyer who would agree to let her live in the house for the rest of her life. That lucky buyer was a Vietnamese businessman, Tran Buu, who purchased the house for $63,000 and gave Mrs. Hill a life-long lease on the street-floor apartment. Her rent was $125 a month with a pledge not to increase it by more than 5 percent each year. Buu moved in upstairs and planned to develop four units, which he would sell one by one upon completion. Because he insisted on high standards of craftsmanship, these condos are among the most attractive and substantial on the block to this day, while many others have had to be redone two or even three times since first being condoized.

#29 HOLYOKE STREET. Cornelia Lee inherited the house from her mother, who bought #29 in early years of the twentieth century. Cornelia's son, George Robinson, grew up on Holyoke in the 1960s and '70s watching as new buyers took advantage of the staggering increase in property values. Eventually George decided to give it a try by making himself general contractor and converting the building to condos himself.

People in the neighborhood knew George as the entrepreneur who sold Christmas trees in the winter and had a fried fish stand outside Charlie's Sandwich Shoppe for a few summers. Everyone hoped for the best but, after relocating his mother and using friends and acquaintances as workmen, the project languished, dragging on as subcontractors bowed out and the city pressed for licensed builders. George finally gave up on the venture and moved away from the street. A new developer took over and, in time, sold the units as condos.

While this transformation of the South End was taking place, two major projects were unfolding along the border facing downtown. Copley Place, a luxury shopping mall located in the Marriott Hotel but connected to the Prudential and the new Westin Hotel by glassed-in bridges, opened in 1983 and became home for such high-end outlets as Neiman Marcus, Gucci, Dior, and Tiffany's. The mall, with its forty-foot waterfall and stone lined rivulets, graces an expansive rotunda that constantly bustles with opulent shoppers and tourists. It stands next door, in a kind of ironic counterpoint, to Tent City where South Enders fought so hard to build low and moderate income housing.

Southwest Corridor Park was the decade's second massive undertaking, a narrow, ninety-acre swath of land extending nearly five miles from the Forest Hills T station in Jamaica Plain to the Back Bay T station on Dartmouth Street. As mentioned in the previous chapter, this long stretch was cleared to make way for an I-95 extension that would go from Route 128 into Boston with a relocated Orange Line going down the

24.

Southwest Corridor Park under construction.

highway's median. Community groups had managed to halt highway construction, but what to do with the cleared land remained a question. Again, countless meetings were held to decide how to proceed. South Enders Ken Kruckemeyer, Ellen Gordon, and Dan Ocasio, now working in various transportation jobs, made sure the park's planning process was open to neighborhood people for their input and ideas. The magnificent new park, with the Orange Line and Amtrak running underneath, was officially opened in 1987. It boasted 11 tot-lot playgrounds, 12 athletic courts, 2 children's spray pools, 2 outdoor performance amphitheaters, 150 community gardens, countless flower beds, and several acres of wide-open green space.

An estimated 38,000 vacant lots existed throughout Boston in the late 1960s. Many South Enders had worked diligently for years to clean up these areas of the neighborhood for gardens and attractive green space. They hauled out mattresses, washing machines, and old televisions, sifted out rotting cigarette packages and liquor "nip" bottles, and tilled the soil to make it usable for planting. Eleanor Strong was a particular hero of this effort. Easily recognized as she biked around the neighborhood, frequently stopping to inspect gardens or pull an unwanted weed in the parks, Eleanor acted as the neighborhood guardian against ingrates who trashed walkways, traipsed through flower beds, or failed to pick up after their dogs. She told me of one occasion when she watched a fire truck almost back over the circular flower bed at the end of West Rutland Square. She praised the men for being careful not to climb the curb, and the fireman told her they wouldn't dare because they knew she would be after them if they did!

Eleanor wanted more than a pretty neighborhood, however. She argued that the real value of parks and gardens was their role in building community life — that they brought people of diverse backgrounds (especially elders and apartment dwellers) together outdoors. Many South Enders came from gardening cultures, she argued, and community gardens helped them keep in touch with past lives. Eleanor lobbied long and hard for urban gardens, resulting in today's twenty open areas with hundreds of individual plots in the South End.

I got my first community garden plot on the Southwest

25

End of Holyoke Street, 2000.

Corridor Park in 1995, and decided one summer day to ask our garden coordinator, Marcie Curry, about the backgrounds of gardeners in our ten-plot designated area. Raised in the Philippines herself, she said, "As I remember just offhand, last year we had an elderly black couple, a gay fitness-center owner, a divorced father with two young sons, a single-woman flight attendant, an elderly handicapped woman, and a housewife."

There have been many artists who have lived in the South End over the years. Among the better known are: Ellen Banks (painter, former resident of Brookline Street); Khalil Gibran (renown painter and sculptor, now deceased, of West Canton Street); Steve Trefonides (painter, formerly of Union Park

Street); Tom Rebek (watercolorist on Washington Street); and Jerry Pinkney (children's books illustrator of Appleton Street.) But the only artist I knew and could see from my Holyoke Street window was Allan Crite.

By the end of the decade (the 1980s) covered in this chapter, almost every house in my area of the South End had been renovated, or gutted and rehabbed. There was one conspicuous exception — #410 Columbus, home and studio of Allan Crite. The storefront on the ground floor had served as office for the Rainbow Party when Mel King ran for mayor in 1983 (a close race which, if won, would have given notoriously racist

26.

Drawing by Allan Crite, St. Stephen's Church, 1978.

Boston its first black mayor), but it had since been boarded up. Not the upstairs! One morning I called and made an appointment to go and visit Allan. I remembered him from the days when I took Sam and Emmy to St. Stephen's. As official artist for the cover of the Sunday bulletin, Allan would often sketch during the service. In fact, I have kept one drawing he did of me and others in the congregation in October 1978.

Despite knowing that Allan had works in the Museum of Fine Arts, the Smithsonian, and elsewhere, I was not prepared for what I would see as I climbed the creaky stairs in #410 Columbus. From the bottom step all the way up, and wall-to-wall throughout every room on floors above, I viewed hundreds of bright paintings and sketches — some, lively scenes of neighborhood people living their daily lives, others on religious themes. Moving slowly and reserved now at age 83, Allan was was not especially eager to talk but did speak of his childhood in the South End — art classes at the Children's Arts Center on Rutland Street and his mother's early encouragement for him to draw and paint. Though accepted at Yale in 1929, he chose to go to the School of Museum of Fine Arts in Boston. He had spent his whole life in the South End, he said, living in the neighborhood and making art. The park where West Canton, Appleton, and Columbus Avenue converge is called Allan Rohan Crite Park in honor of his work and contribution to the community.

In the decade to come, the last one in a stretch of 200 years since Boston City Council voted to fill in the Neck, the South

End had endured. But in the last decade of the twentieth century, the neighborhood seemed to go through yet another dramatic change. The next chapter tells what happened — and why.

Holyoke's New Era

1990 – 2000

In the early 1990s a house on Holyoke Street sold for $250,000–$300,000. By the end of that decade, the same house sold for over $1 million. This fact, more than any others, reflects the change on Holyoke and the South End during the last decade of the twentieth century. A neighborhood once occupied by laborers and shopkeepers was now home to lawyers, stock-brokers, company executives, consultants, and venture capitalists as the American economy boomed. The change on the street seemed staggering at times.

By the time I started writing this chapter I had become a regular at MIT's Rotch Library. I found a relatively recent and very valuable document called *Save Our City: A Case for*

Boston, published in 1992 by Historic Boston, Incorporated and co-written by several South End authors whose names I recognized: Eugenie Beal, Arthur Howe, Susan Park, and others who had been involved with the South End Historical Society. The study focused almost entirely on economic issues facing the city at the outset of a new century, specifically how the preservation of private properties and restoration of neighborhoods created jobs for community people and boosted local business by encouraging tourism. The perspective had shifted away from the old issues of low income housing, big construction projects, and even improved schools. It was definitely a sign of the times.

I became part of the shift myself. When my children were off to college in the mid-1990s, I began to look at my house with a new eye. We had lived as a family with tenants, relatives, friends, and friends of friends since I bought it in 1978. In fact, I kept a list of people who came and went over the years: forty-three people had rented rooms upstairs, and seven had rented the street-floor apartment. The first tenant was a taxi driver with a wooden leg; others included a teacher of English as a Second Language, a folk singer, an aspiring ballet dancer, a housewife who wanted to escape from her husband, a fashion model out of work, a Brazilian plastic surgeon, a Chinese waitress, an Israeli soldier, a Filipino computer salesman, a student from the Ivory Coast, an architect from Odessa working on Boston's Third Harbor Tunnel, and many more.

In the summer of 1997, I emptied out the house and turned it over to a young Brazilian carpenter, Cesar Paiva, to be general contractor. He was only twenty-four years old but I had used him for smaller jobs and could see he was an excellent problem-solver and a highly skilled carpenter. Moving across the street to a basement room that Joe Linkin occasionally rented at #24 Holyoke, I was out of the house for approximately ten months while Cesar remade my house, using mostly Brazilian compatriots as plasterers, tile-layers, carpenters and painters. Realtors told me later the workmanship was superb, making the units easy to rent. Each of the top two floors became sunny one-bedroom apartments, with tiled kitchen and small French-door entrances to a study off the living room. The parlor floor, street floor, and basement became a triplex, with the old woodwork and wainscoting preserved wherever possible, but with new oak floors in the bedrooms and Mexican tiles throughout the office and basement furnace room. Cesar, by the way, went on to establish his own very successful business, working in Greater Boston and Brazil. In 2002 he took me with his wife and son to meet the whole Paiva family in Victoria, Brazil, where he was just finishing his first apartment building. Among the many treats of that trip was a visit to the Pantanal, the largest inland wetlands in the world — back then still undiscovered by the tourist industry.

The tenants who rented the new apartments were representative of 1990s South Enders. Among the earliest was a gay couple who had merged households for the first time — one a vice president at Fidelity and the other a human service worker at an agency on Beacon Hill. Others included an

Egyptian student at Harvard Business School, a stock broker who drove a motorcycle, a German cardiologist and his family, and a young lawyer. Bankers and stockbrokers followed.

Of course, to satisfy the expectations of homeowners now paying some of the city's highest taxes, the municipal government had to make improvements in the South End. The upgrade of street lights was a case in point. In the late 1960s, the Department of Public Works installed new lighting on Holyoke — ugly cement poles extending long bony arms to cast a bluish fluorescent light over the sidewalks. In 1980, these were replaced by a large lollipop-shaped globes giving off a pinkish tone. In 1997, as Holyoke became a truly gentrified street, the city replaced the lollipops with acorn style lamps which were a close facsimile of the antique-looking gaslights on Beacon Hill.

Sidewalks followed a similar pattern, initially improved as a result of the transportation plan spearheaded by South Enders back in the 1960s. The old cracked and broken cement walks, with their blacktop patches, were replaced with new brick sidewalks in the early 1980s. Around the same time the city carved out small plots every seven yards or so to plant ash trees. The branches extending out over the street became a graceful archway in the 1990s, shading and softening the look of the street from early spring to late autumn.

Backyards and alleys changed as well. When I moved to Holyoke Street, backyards were largely neglected, except by people like Geri Sinclair who were serious gardeners. Because light is interrupted by the shadows of houses as the sun moves east to west, grass and flowers don't do well. Most people ignored their yards, using them mostly for storing tools, old furniture, and an occasional automobile. That ended when condo conversion came, leading to three or four residents per building and multiplying the automobile population exponentially. Gradually, the alley looked more like a downtown parking lot than backyard dumping and storage area. Condominium owners and renters started using all the land behind their houses to park vehicles, sometimes lining up one behind another. In 1996 a developer added a townhouse at the end of West Canton, filling a vacant lot where a building had fallen down decades earlier, which I could see kitty-corner from my parlor windows. That house, composed of three large, luxury apartments, had a blacktopped parking area with bright yellow lines, supermarket style. The yard consisted of a patch of ivy and one tiny shrub.

The cars themselves were almost always the latest models. In the past, cars parked in the Holyoke Street alley tended to be older ones, kept for years until they rusted out. The 1990s cars were brand new, sports cars, jeep-type station wagons and vans, and SUVs. My new next-door neighbor was a single woman who bought an upper-floor condominium at #15; when she first moved in, she parked a BMW sports convertible out back. One morning she pulled up to the front of the house in a new Nissan Infiniti. I watched as she brought down a ten-speed bicycle and loaded it into the hatchback of the car. She still had the BMW, but it couldn't carry a bicycle for a ride in the country.

Changes in newcomers' financial assets inevitably meant change for many of the long-standing stores and businesses in the community. The old Venice Lounge, a favorite drinking place for retired black men of the neighborhood, closed down; it reopened as Anchovies, a tiny restaurant and bar decorated in collectibles (tin airplanes, a carousel horse, a deer head, a mobile made of melted plastic bottles) and catering to single professionals. I happened to be walking down Columbus when workmen were taking down the six-foot-long sign above the original bar. Large bold lettering on a dirty white plastic background read: VENICE LOUNGE, LADIES WELCOME. I asked the workmen if I could have it to give to my teenage son for Christmas. Sam still has it, though it's now stored in my Holyoke basement.

The shoe repair and produce shop next to the new Anchovies went through many hands before becoming Giacomo's, an Italian restaurant with hand-painted wall murals and valet parking. Up in the next block, where the federal Head Start program for children of low-income families used to be, a succession of enterprises moved in: a drycleaner, a hair salon, a local insurance agency, and a large convenience market, the South End Emporium. Some of these have already moved on.

Over the years the only establishment around Holyoke Street, indeed one of the few in the South End, that has remained virtually unchanged is Charlie's Sandwich Shoppe. Greek immigrant Charlie Poulis opened the restaurant in 1927 and was bought out three years later by his assistant Chris Manjorides, whose sons, Arthur and Chris, still run the place. Arthur recalled, "My father died in 1995, but he was the real heart of the business for all those years. Charlie would work from 6:00 A.M. to 6:00 P.M., and my dad would work the night twelve hours. It was in those hours the he baked the cornbread muffins, breads and pies that helped make Charlie's reputation as a great place for breakfast and lunches. My dad used to sell fifty dozen muffins a day back then, two for a nickel."

Then, as now, the restaurant had a flair for atmosphere, including ten birdcages lining the walls of the restaurant (two birds each) for years. In the 1950s at Thanksgiving time, the Manjorides kept live turkeys in the front windows until one got out and started flying over the heads of the customers. For

27.

Charlie's Sandwich Shoppe.

a while there was an aquarium on the counter with goldfish; someone stole the fish and later returned them, but the aquarium didn't last much longer after that. Today the Manjorides brothers do the cooking behind the counter and sisters, Fontaine and Marie, wait on tables. With black and white tile floors, photos of family and friends everywhere (even on the back of the cash register), a phalanx of stainless steel stools, and a corner hand sink, Charlie's has the ambiance of another era — one that neighbors and tourists seem to love. On warm summer Saturdays lines reach halfway down the block.

Traditionally South Enders have thought of their "neighborhood" as the street where they live, or maybe that street and a few others. People in these various enclaves began to form associations in the 1940s to address pressing concerns or desired improvements. When I moved to Holyoke I learned my street belonged to the Cosmopolitan Neighborhood Association. A neighbor on Braddock Park met me one afternoon in the alley between our streets to hand me a shoebox full of old member lists and meeting notes. They were sketchy, but verified that garbage collection had been one shared concern, for sure. Over the years I learned of other South End groups: Ellis, Pilot Block, Eight Streets, and ones farther down near Washington Street. Many had been a powerful force during the urban renewal years.

In the 1990s our Cosmopolitan Association came to the fore again. Nina Garfinkle, who owned a condominium at #7 Holyoke, had been robbed three times after she took occupancy in 1987 — once the thieves made off with almost everything she owned. Nina turned to the Cosmopolitan Neighborhood Association for help and soon a street watch was organized. According to plan, teams of four or five Holyokers would walk up and down the street and through the alleys several times a week. Drug dealers had a presence in the neighborhood, people had observed, and many believed the young bike riders zipping up and down the alleys were being directed by cellphone to deliver drugs to buyers coming in from the suburbs. This was a worry as well.

Barry Hinckley was young and recently married when he moved to #24 Holyoke in 1995. Soon after settling in, his wife Heather, who worked as a bicycle messenger, had her bike stolen from in front of the house. In addition to break-ins, Barry learned, there had been twelve muggings on the Southwest Corridor between December 1995 and March 1996. After a couple of crime-watch meetings, Barry decided to get involved by giving everyone his e-mail address so people could send him reports about crime on the street. To promote the network he organized two block parties with donated hamburgers and beer. Charlie's Sandwich Shoppe provided a lot of the food and almost everyone on the block showed up, including many elderly residents who didn't have computers, much less online experience. Pretty soon Barry was spending two to three hours a night answering notes and missives from neighbors. The *Boston Globe* picked up the story, calling the venture the first "Internet Neighborhood Crime Watch" in the country. By the time Barry left the South End in 1997, he'd been contacted by Philadelphia, Minneapolis, and

Cleveland for information about his Holyoke Street project. West Canton residents David Yip and Nina Garfinkle kept the program going until around 1998.

Todd Davis, a software small-business owner, had moved to the South End in 1991. Hearing about Holyoke's online crime-watch communications, Todd decided to establish a website to include the whole South End. By summer of 1998, it was up and running as the South End Forum with a tag line, "Best Neighborhood in Boston." Very soon it was receiving 250 "hits" a day.

The South End has been known to have a strong and visible gay community since the late 1960s. The June 2000 *South End News* ran a front page article about the community saying gay individuals were, in fact, the "first" to discover the area as a potentially attractive place to live. Certainly many gay individuals (among them Arthur DuCharme who bought several worn-down houses and sold them to people who saw their aesthetic value) moved to the South End before it became gentrified. Al Rondeau, who opened his real estate office in 1965, was another pioneering gay.

Franco Campanello came to the South End in 1974, purchased the Metropolitan Health Club on Columbus and Berkeley Streets, and bought a condominium at #16 Holyoke Street in 1995. Franco said gays came to the South End early because, without children, they were less worried about safety and schools, and therefore more willing to take chances on risky areas. Besides, the South End was near downtown gay clubs and had "somewhat" of a reputation for tolerance. When the gay baby boomers came of age in the 1970s, Franco said, many flocked to the cities for professional jobs. The South End was a convenient place to live, with a gay network already in place.

The South End Emporium is another example of diversity the South End has sustained even as the neighborhood became an expensive place to live. Wandossan Alemu Desta came to the United States in 1981 from Ethiopia when he was seventeen. In 1992 he purchased a 3,000-square-foot storefront on Columbus Avenue at the corner of West Newton Street. Al employed several family members and they went to work stocking the shelves. Today the store carries twenty kinds of coffee beans, and more than forty spices and products from Ethiopia and other East African countries in addition to fresh vegetables, ready-made sandwiches, and a vast array of everyday grocery items. Neighborhood people use the store on a regular basis.

One treasured South End institution did not survive. On July 16, 2000, more than sixty people gathered in the basement of the Union United Methodist Church at the corner of Columbus and Braddock for a potluck dinner of pizza, baked chicken, and soft drinks to mark the end of the Braddock Drug Store. This old South End classic finally closed, owner Bob Sterling reported, because it couldn't compete with big chains such as CVS and Walgreens. Hundreds of South Enders — both residents and those who had moved away — remember its steadfast presence. Children from Concord Baptist remember sneaking in to buy hand-scooped ice cream between Sunday school and church; mothers remember the racks that held cards, ribbon, and plastic toys for a late-notice party; and old men remember it as the one place where they could get a cold beer on Sunday (under the counter, in those days). Others hail back to the times they bought a handful of fresh cashews or pistachios in a small white bag, or a supply of paper towels, toilet paper, or even dish cloths. I depended on the Braddock for Christmas tree lights, Halloween candy, paper grass for Easter baskets, and over-the-counter medicine.

The Braddock Drug Store remained empty for a couple of years, until a mortgage company rented the space, put in carpeting, hung prints on the walls, installed computers, and opened the doors for new home buyers. A new century had begun. Some customers would become condominium buyers; some, like two couples on Holyoke, would be planning to turn the row houses back into single family homes, as they were when first built. It would take a few million dollars to pull off the restoration, but they were determined to recover the glory of the original Victorian bow fronts. In at least one way, Holyoke seems to have come full circle.

NOTES

CHAPTER I

1. Margaret Supplee Smith, "Between City and Suburb: Architecture and Planning in Boston's South End" (PhD. diss., Brown University, 1976), 24–43.

2. Smith, *Between City and Suburb*, 77–78.

3. Lawrence W. Kennedy, *Planning the City Upon a Hill* (Amherst: University of Massachusetts, 1992), 52.

4. Kennedy, *Planning the City*, 58.

5. Walter Muir Whitehill, *Boston: A Topographical History*, 2nd ed. (Cambridge, Mass.: Belknap Press of Harvard University Press, 1968), 78.

6. Robert Campbell and Peter Vanderwarker, *Cityscapes of Boston* (Boston: Houghton Mifflin, 1992), 78.

7. Whitehill, *Boston*, 104.

8. Edwin M. Bacon, *Book of Boston: Fifty Years' Recollections of the New England Metropolis* (Boston: Book of Boston Company, 1916), 102–103.
9. Whitehill, *Boston,* 98–102.

CHAPTER 2

1. Smith, *Between City and Suburb,* 71–73.
2. William F. Robinson, *Abandoned New England* (New York: New York Graphic Society, 1976), 130–131.
3. Douglass Shand-Tucci, *Built in Boston: City and Suburb 1800–1950* (Amherst: University of Massachusetts Press, 1988), 103.

CHAPTER 3

1. Whitehill, *Boston,* 112.
2. Kennedy, *Planning the City,* 57–58. Also Campbell and Vanderwarker, *Cityscapes,* 190.
3. Matt "Uno" Regan, "Annihilation of the South End" (personal essay, n.d.), 3.
4. Campbell and Vanderwarker, *Cityscapes,* 142–43.
5. Sam B. Warner Jr., *Streetcar Suburbs* (Cambridge, Mass.: Joint Center for Urban Studies of Massachusetts Institute for Technology and Harvard University, 1962), 14–23.

6. Matthew Edel, Elliot Sclar, and Daniel Luris, *Shakey Places: Homeownership and Social Mobility in Boston's Suburbanization* (New York: Columbia University Press, 1984), 83.

7. William Dean Howells, *The Rise of Silas Lapham* (New York: Penguin Books USA, 1986), 24.

8. John Marquand, *The Late George Apley* (Boston: Little, Brown and Co.), 27–28.

9. Thomas H. O'Connor, *The Boston Irish* (Boston: Northeastern University Press, 1995), 239.

10. There is also evidence on maps and tax records that Anne F. Damon held the property for a while. Margaret Supplee Smith writes that Stubbs sold to Annie Hope in 1869 but I did not find her name when I traced the deeds. Perhaps Stubbs sold to Theresa and Charlotte first but they couldn't make payments and sold back to Stubbs, who then sold to Rosy Wiel.

CHAPTER 4

1. O'Connor, *The Boston Irish*, 152.

2. Albert Benedict Wolfe, *The Lodging House Problem in Boston* (Boston: Houghton Mifflin, 1906),14.

3. Whitehill, *Boston*, 137.

4. Wolfe, *The Lodging House Problem*, 1–7.

5. Wolfe, *The Lodging House Problem*, 98.

6. *The South End* (Boston: Boston 200 Corporation, 1975), 3–4.

7. Mary Antin, *The Promised Land* (New York: Random House Inc.), 242.

8. Eleanor Woods, *Robert A. Woods: Champion of Democracy* (Boston: Houghton Mifflin), 25–26.

9. This movement actually began in England but was instituted in several cities in the United States, mostly notably in Chicago where Jane Adams and Ellen Gates Starr established Hull House in 1889.

10. Robert Woods, *The City Wilderness: A Settlement Study by Residents and Associates of the South End House* (Boston: Houghton Mifflin, 1989), 265–270.

11. Woods, *City Wilderness,* 32.

12. Woods, *City Wilderness,* 98.

13. Woods, *City Wilderness,* 154.

14. Woods, *City Wilderness,* 170–177.

15. Woods, *City Wilderness,* 120–122.

16. Woods, *City Wilderness,* 176–199.

17. Woods, *City Wilderness,* 170.

18. Woods, *City Wilderness,* 159–164.

19. Woods, *City Wilderness,* 125.

20. Alvan Sanborn, *Moody's Lodging House and Other Tenement Sketches* (Boston: Copeland and Day, 1985),135–137.

21. Helen Howe, *Gentle Americans 1864–1960: Biography of a Breed* (New York: Harper and Row, 1965), 269–270.

22. Whitehill, *Boston,* 131.

CHAPTER 5

1. Orpheus M. McAdoo and Mattie Allen McAdoo
   Papers. Beinecke Rare Book and Manuscript Library,
   Yale University Library. http://hdl.handle.net/10079/fa/
   beinecke.mcadoo.
2. Adelaide M. Cromwell, *The Other Brahmins* (Fayetteville,
   University of Arkansas Press, 1994), 115–116.

CHAPTER 6

1. Paul Benzaquin, *Holocaust,* 138.
2. Walter Firey, *Land Use in Central Boston* (Cambridge,
   Mass.: Harvard University Press, 1947), 305.
3. Kennedy, *Planning the City,* 158.
4. Michael Conzen and George Lewis. *Boston: A Geographical
   Portrait.* (Cambridge, Mass.: Ballinger Publishing Co.,
   1976), 50.
5. Richard Bolan, *South End Report* (Boston Redevelopment
   Authority, 1962), 63.
6. Bolan, *South End Report,* 11.
7. Bolan, *South End Report,* 76.
8. Bolan, *South End Report,* 63–68.
9. John Sacco is fondly remembered as the author of the
   South End News "Police Report" column that ran from
   1980–2000.

CHAPTER 7

1. In the last months of her illness, Virginia asked Mel King if he would visit to discuss her will. She had decided to give her house to the black community that had once flourished on Holyoke Street. Following their discussion, Virginia decided to bequeath the now million-dollar house to the League of Women for Community Services, Inc., a black women's service club on Massachusetts Avenue. When Mel went to see Virginia while the paperwork was being done, she asked him again why he had sold her the house. Thin and frail when she related the story to me, she nevertheless laughed heartily when she told me he said he had wanted to "integrate" the neighborhood.

2. *South End: District Profile — Proposed 1979–81.* (Boston: Boston Redevelopment Authority, 1979), 5.

3. Frederick Pikielek. *Boston's South End: Past and Present* (Boston: Boston Redevelopment Authority, 1974), 76.

4. Michael P. Conzen and George K. Lewis. *Boston: A Geographical Portrait* (Cambridge: Ballinger Publishing Co., 1976), 64.

CHAPTER 8

1. O'Connor, *The Boston Irish,* 210–217.

2. Thomas H. O'Connor, *Building a New Boston: Politics and Urban Renewal 1950–1970* (Boston: Northeastern

University Press, 1993), 126.

3. O'Connor, *Building a New Boston,* 124.

4. Kennedy, *Planning the City,*159–161.

5. O'Conner, *Building a New Boston,* 147.

6. Kennedy, *Planning the City,* 171–172.

7. O'Connor, *Building a New Boston,* 174–178.

8. Kennedy, *Planning the City,* 178–182.

9. Kennedy, *Planning the City,* 186–188.

10. Kennedy, *Planning the City,* 228–232.

11. Mel King, *Chain of Change* (Boston: South End Press, 1979), 64–70.

12. Barry Bluestone and Mary Huff Stevenson, *The Boston Renaissance: Race, Space and Economic Change in an American Metropolis* (New York: Russell Sage Foundation, 2000), 88.

13. King, *Chain of Change,* 111–113.

14. Peter Medoff and Holly Sklar, *Streets of Hope* (Boston: South End Press, 1994), 20–21.

15. *South End Transit and Traffic Proposal.* (Boston: South End Committee on Transportation, 1972), 1.

CHAPTER 9

1. O'Connor, *The Boston Irish,* 257–260.

2. J. Anthony Lukas, *Common Ground: A Turbulent Decade in the Lives of Three American Families* (New York: Alfred A. Knopf, 1985), 556–651.

3. Wright, *The South End on My Mind,* (Privately printed, Boston, 2000), 10.
4. Sunday mornings, the city let cars to park on the Columbus Avenue meridian from Clarendon Street almost to Massachusetts Avenue in an effort to accommodate suburban churchgoers.

CHAPTER 10

1. *South End Profile.* (Boston Redevelopment Authority Research Department, 1988), 8.

PICTURES SOURCES

BIBLIOGRAPHY

Antin, Mary. *The Promised Land*. New York: Random House Inc., 2001.

Bacon, Edwin M. *Book of Boston: Fifty Years' Recollections of the New England Metropolis*. Boston: Book of Boston Company, 1916.

Barak, Gregg. *Gimme Shelter: A Social History of Homelessness in Contemporary America*. New York: Praeger, 1991.

Barnet, Alison. "One Woman's Hands." *Glue*, March/April 1998.

Baum, Alice and Donald Burnes. *A Nation in Denial: The Truth about Homelessness.* Boulder: Westview Press, 1993.

Benzaquin, Paul. *Holocaust!* New York: Henry Holt and Co., 1959.

Bernardi, Dria. *Houses with Names.* Chicago: University of Illinois Press, 1990.

Bluestone, Barry and Mary Huff Stevenson. *The Boston Renaissance: Race, Space and Economic Change in an American Metropolis*. New York: Russell Sage Foundation, 2000.

Boer, Albert. *The Development of USES, a Chronology of the United South End Settlements, 1891–1966*. Boston: USES, 1966.

Bolan, Richard. *South End Report*. Boston: Boston Redevelopment Authority, October 1962.

Boston: The Way It Was. Boston: WGBH Education Fund, 1996.

Brand, Stewart. *How Buildings Learn*. New York: Penguin Books, 1994.

Brown, Jeffrey. *Profile of Boston 1929–1980*. Boston: Boston Redevelopment Authority, 1982.

Burt, Martha. *Over the Edge: The Growth of Homelessness in the 1980s*. New York: Russell Sage Foundation, 1992.

Bushee, Frederick A. *Ethnic Factors in the Population of Boston*. New York: Arno Press and the New York Times, 1970.

Campbell, Robert and Peter Vanderwarker. *Cityscapes of Boston*. Boston: Houghton Mifflin, 1992.

Carlson, Stephen P. with Thomas W. Harding. *From Boston to the Berkshires*. Boston: Boston Street Railway Association, Inc., 1990.

City of Boston. *City Document No.3 The Sewerage of Boston: A Report by a Commission Consisting of E. S. Chesbrough, C.E., Moses Lane, C.E, and Charles F. Folsom. M.D.*, 1875.

Clarke, Eliot C. *Main Drainage Works of the City of Boston*. Boston: Rockwell and Churchill, City Printers, 1885.

Commercial and Financial New England. Boston: Boston Herald Publisher, 1986.

Conzen, Michael P. and George K. Lewis. *Boston: A Geographical Portrait*. Cambridge, Mass.: Ballinger Publishing Co., 1976.

Cromwell, Adelaide M. *The Other Brahmins: Boston's Black Upper Class 1750–1950*. Fayetteville: University of Arkansas Press, 1994.

Daniels, John. *In Freedom's Birthplace: A Study of the Boston Negroes.* Boston and New York: Houghton Mifflin, 1914.

Domosh, Mona. *Invented Cities: The Creation of Landscape in Nineteenth-Century New York and Boston*. New Haven: Yale University Press, 1996.

Drake, St.Clair and Horace Cayton. *Black Metropolis: A Study of Negro Life in a Northern City*. New York: Harper and Row, 1962.

Edel, Matthew, Elliott Sclar, and Daniel Luria. *Shaky Palaces: Homeownership and Social Mobility in Boston's Suburban- ization.* New York: Columbia University Press, 1984.

Firey, Walter. *Land Use in Central Boston.* Cambridge, Mass.: Harvard University Press, 1947.

Fitch, James Marston. *American Building: the Historical Forces that Shaped It*. 2nd ed. New York: Schocken Books, 1973 (reprint of Vol. 1 published by Houghton Mifflin, 1966–1972).

Formisano, Ronald P. and Constance K. Burns, eds. *Boston 1700–1980: The Evolution of Urban Politics.* Westport, Conn.: Greenwood Press, 1984.

Gans, Herbert J. *The Urban Villagers: Group and Class in the Life of Italian-Americans*. New York: The Free Press, 1962.

Green, James R. *The South End*. Boston: Boston 200 Corp., 1975.

Gross, Ernie. *American Years: A Chronology of United States History.* New York: Scribner, 1999.

Hale, Edward Everett. *Historic Boston and Its Neighborhoods*. New York: Appleton and Co., 1898.

Handlin, Oscar. *Boston's Immigrants 1790–1880*. Cambridge, Mass.: Harvard University Press, 1991.

Hareven, Tamara K. and Maris Vinovskis. "Marital Fertility, Ethnicity, and Occupation in Urban Families: An Analysis of South Boston and the South End in 1880." *Journal of Social History*, Spring 1975.

Higgins, George V. *Style Versus Substance: Boston, Kevin White and the Politics of Illusion*. New York: Macmillan, 1984.

Hirsch, Kathleen. *A Home in the Heart of the City*. New York: North Point Press, 1998.

Holleran, Michael. *Boston's Changeful Times: Origins of Preservation and Planning in America*. Baltimore: Johns Hopkins Press, 1998.

Horton, James Oliver and Lois Horton. *Black Bostonians: Family Life and Community Struggle in the Antebellum North*. New York: Holmes and Meier Publishers, 1979.

Howe, Helen. *The Gentle Americans 1864–1960: Biography of a Breed.* New York: Harper and Row, 1965.

Howells, William Dean. *The Rise of Silas Lapham.* New York: Penguin Books USA, 1986 (first published by Tichnor and Company, 1885).

Jacobs, Donald Martin. "A History of the Boston Negro from the Revolution to the Civil War." PhD. diss., Brown University, 1968.

Jacobs, Jane. *Life and Death of American Cities.* New York: Random House, 1961.

Jennings, James and Mel King, editors. *From Access to Power: Black Politics in Boston.* Rochester, Vt.: Schenkman Books, 1986.

Johnson, Allen and Malone Dumas, eds. *Dictionary of American Biography, Vol II.* New York: Charles Scribner's and Sons, 1929.

Kay, Jane Holtz. *Lost Boston.* Boston: Houghton Mifflin, 1980.

Kennedy, Lawrence W. *Planning the City Upon a Hill.* Amherst: University of Massachusetts, 1992.

King, Mel. *Chain of Change.* Boston: South End Press, 1979.

Knights, Peter R. *The Plain People of Boston 1830–1860.* New York: Oxford University Press, 1971.

Koren, John. *Boston, 1822–1922 The Story of Its Government and Principal Activities.* Boston: City of Boston Printing Department, 1923.

Krieger, Alex, David Cobb and Amy Turner. *Mapping Boston.* Turner, eds. The Muriel G. and Norman B. Leventhal Family Foundation. Boston: MIT Press,1999.

Laws and Ordinances: 1860. Boston: City of Boston, 1864.

Lukas, J. Anthony. *Common Ground: A Turbulent Decade in the*

Lives of Three American Families. New York: Alfred A. Knopf, 1985.

Lupo, Alan, Frank Colcord, Edmund P. Fowler. *Rites of Way: The Politics of Transportation in Boston and the U.S. City*. Boston: Little Brown and Co., 1971.

Lyndon, Donlyn. *The City Observed: Boston*. New York: Random House, 1982.

Marchione, William. "Railroads engineered great growth for early Boston." *Boston Tab*, May 4–10, 1999.

———. "The year of the railroads." *Boston Tab*, April 27–May 3, 1999.

Maril, Nadja. *American Lighting: 1840–1940*. West Chester, Pa.: Schiffer Publishing, 1989.

Marquand, John. *The Late George Apley*. Boston: Little, Brown and Co., 1936.

McAdoo, Orpheus M. and Mattie Allen McAdoo, Papers. Beinecke Rare Book and Manuscript Library, Yale University Library. http://hdl.handle.net/10079/fa/beinecke.mcadoo

Medoff, Peter and Holly Sklar. *Streets of Hope*. Boston: South End Press, 1994.

Merwin, Henry Childs. "The Irish in American Life." *Atlantic Monthly*, March 1896.

Mumford, Lewis. *The City in History*. New York: Harcourt, Brace & World, 1961.

Myers, Denys. *Gaslighting in America: A Guide for Historic Preservation*. Washington D.C.: U.S. Department of the Interior, 1978.

Neale, John. "Two Squares Come Full Circle." *South End News*,
    February 25, 1999.

Neill, Alexander Sutherland. New York: Hart Publishing
    Company, 1962.

O'Brien, Margaret C. *Diversity and Change in Boston's
    Neighborhoods: A Comparison of Demographic, Social, and
    Economic Characteristics and Housing, 1970–1980.* Boston:
    Boston Redevelopment Authority Research Department,
    1985.

O'Connor, Thomas H. *Bibles, Brahmins and Bosses.* 2nd ed.
    Boston: Trustees of the Boston Public Library, 1984.

———. *Building a New Boston: Politics and Urban Renewal
    1950–1970.* Boston: Northeastern University Press, 1993.

———. *The Boston Irish.* Boston: Northeastern University
    Press, 1995.

Patrick, Seán. *Patrick's Corner.* Gretna, La.: Pelican Publishing,
    1992.

Pikielek, Frederick. *Boston's South End: Past and Present.* Boston:
    Boston Redevelopment Authority Research Department,
    1974.

Primack, Mark, ed. *Greening of Boston.* Boston: Boston
    Foundation, 1987.

Prindle, Elizabeth. "Remembrance of Things Jazz: A History
    of the South End's Jazz Clubs." *South End Historical Society
    Newsletter* 30:2, October 2002.

Regan, Matt "Uno." "Annihilation of the South End." Personal
    essay, n.d.

Robinson, William F. *Abandoned New England.* New York:

New York Graphic Society, 1976.

Rodwin, Lloyd. *Housing and Economic Progress*. Cambridge, Mass.: Harvard University Press and the Technology Press, 1961.

Ross, Marjorie Drake. *The Book of Boston: Victorian Period 1837–1901*. New York: Hastings House, 1964.

Sammarco, Anthony Mitchell. *Images of America: Boston A Century of Progress*. Dover, N.H.: Arcadia Publishing, 1995.

Sanborn, Alvan Francis. *Moody's Lodging House and Other Tenement Sketches*. Boston: Copeland and Day, 1895.

Sanborn, George M. *A Chronicle of the Boston Transit System*. Boston: State Transportation Library, 1992.

Schurtleff, Nathaniel Bradstreet. *A Topographical and Historical Description of Boston*, 3rd ed. Common Council, 1891.

Seasholes, Nancy, David Cobb, David Bosse, Amy Turner, and Alex Kreiger. Mapping Boston. Cambridge, MA: Massachusetts Institute of Technology Press, 1999.

Shand-Tucci, Douglass. *Boston Bohemia 1881–1900*. Amherst: University of Massachusetts Press, 1995.

———. *Built in Boston: City and Suburb 1800–1950*. Amherst: University of Massachusetts Press, 1988.

Simonds, Thomas. *History of South Boston*. New York: Arno Press, 1974.

Smith, Margaret Supplee. "Between City and Suburb: Architecture and Planning in Boston's South End." PhD. diss., Brown University, 1976.

Smith, Margaret Supplee and John C. Moorhouse.
    "Architecture and the Housing Market: Nineteenth
    Century Row Housing in Boston's South End." *Journal of
    the Society of Architectural Historians* 52, no. 2 (June 1993):
    159–178.

Snow, Caleb H. *History of Boston*. Boston: Abel Bowen,
    1828.

Social Facts by Census. Boston: United Community Services
    of Metropolitan Boston, 1954.

The South End. Boston 200 Neighborhood History Series.
    Boston: Boston 200 Corporation, 1975.

*The South End. Density Impact Study and Zoning
    Recommendations*. Boston: Boston Redevelopment
    Authority, 1988.

South End Transit and Traffic Proposal. Boston: South End
    Committee on Transportation, 1972.

South End: District Profile — Proposed 1979–81. Boston: Boston
    Redevelopment Authority, 1979.

The South End: District Study Committee Report. Boston: Boston
    Landmark Commission, 1983.

State of Homelessness in the City of Boston: Winter 1988. Boston:
    Emergency Shelter Commission, 1988.

Tinory, Eugene P. *Journey from Ammeah, The Story of a Lebanese
    Immigrant*. Brattleboro, Mass.: Amana Books, 1986.

Vernon, Raymond. *The Myth and Reality of Our Urban Problems*.
    Cambridge, Mass.: Joint Center for Urban Studies at
    the Massachusetts Institute of Technology and Harvard
    University, 1962.

von Hoffman, Alexander. *Local Attachments: The Making of an American Urban Neighborhood, 1850 to 1920*. Baltimore: The Johns Hopkins University Press, 1994.

Ward, David. "Nineteenth Century Boston: A Study in the Role of Antecedent and Adjacent Conditions in the Spatial Aspects of Urban Growth." PhD. diss., University of Wisconsin, 1983. Ann Arbor, Mich.: University Microfilms.

Warner, Sam B., Jr. Preface to *The Zone of Emergence* by Robert Woods and Albert Kennedy. 2nd ed. Boston: MIT Press, 1962.

———. *Streetcar Suburbs*. Cambridge, Mass.: Joint Center for Urban Studies of Massachusetts Institute for Technology and Harvard University, 1962.

———. *The Way We Live: Social Change in Metropolitan Boston*. Boston: Trustees of the Public Library, 1977.

Weston, George F. Jr. *Boston Ways*. Boston: Beacon Press, 1957.

Whitehill, Walter Muir. *Boston: A Topographical History*. 2nd ed. Cambridge, Mass.: Belknap Press of Harvard University Press, 1968.

Whittlesey, Robert B. *The South End Row House*. Boston: Report on Low-income Housing Demonstration Project, 1969.

Who Was Who in America. Vol. IV. Chicago: Marquis Who's Who, Inc., 1968.

Whyte, William Foote. *Street Corner Society*. Chicago: University of Chicago Press, 1943.

Wolfe, Albert Benedict. *The Lodging House Problem in Boston.*
    Boston: Houghton Mifflin, 1906.

Womble, Peter. "The Neighborhood Autonomy Movement."
    Senior Honors Thesis, Harvard University, 1970.

Woods, Eleanor H. *Robert A. Woods: Champion of Democracy.*
    Boston: Houghton Mifflin, 1929.

Woods, Robert A., ed. *The City Wilderness: A Settlement Study
    by Residents and Associates of the South End House.* Boston:
    Houghton, Mifflin, 1898.

Wright, Paul. *The South End on My Mind.* Privately printed.
    Boston, 2000.

Yule, Don. "Cooking and Heating the 19th Century Way."
    The Old-House Journal IV: 9, September 1976.

Zeitlin, Morris. *American Cities.* New York: International
    Publishers, 1990.

INTERVIEWS

Alison Barnet

John Bassett

Carolyn Ann Boehne

Gene Boehne

Duncan Bolt

Jane Bowers

Franco Campanello

Richard Card

Arthur Cook

Allan Crite

Donna Crowley

Marcelina Curry

Todd Davis

Winnie Deare

Wandossan Alemu Desta

Adrian duCille

Fran Duffy

Bill and Tako Dwyer

Tom and Geri Ford

Nina Garfinkle

Ruth Ginsberg

Virginia Glennon

Ena Harris

Robert Hathaway

Claire Hayes

Ann Hershfang

Harold Hill

Benjamin Barrett Hinckley III

Cyndi Koebert

Ann Kruckemeyer

Kate Kruckemeyer

Ken Kruckemeyer

Mozel Kyle

Joseph Linkin

Alexis Lugo

Arthur Manjourides

George Maryadas

Tina McCusker

Max Moore

Alan Morris

Carla Nelson

Dan Ocasio

Lloyd Parham

Ruth Parham

Teri Putnam

John Sacco

Edie Schroeder

Kirt Schulte

Nancy Seasholes

Elizabeth Seifel

Geri Sinclair

Barbara Sittinger

Barbara Spears

Jeffrey Stonberg

Eleanor Strong

Furman Walls

Andrea Watkins

B Wolbach

Holister Young

SOURCES VISITED

Boston Athenæum
Boston Buildings Department
Boston Landmarks Commission
Boston Public Library
Boston Redevelopment Authority
Bostonian Society
Massachusetts Historical Society
Massachusetts State Archives
National Archives, Waltham, Massachusetts
Rotch Library, Massachusetts Institute of Technology
State Library of Massachusetts
State Library of Transportation
Suffolk County Courthouse (Boston Registry of Deeds)
South End Historical Society
Simmons College Archives
United South End Settlements
Wellesley College Archives

ACKNOWLEDGEMENTS

•

So many neighbors, friends, and professionals helped me with this book, I hardly know where to begin thanking everyone. I have listed those who shared their time for interviews, but there were many who contributed experiences and information that I may have failed to acknowledge.

First I wish to thank my dear friends, Louise Herman, Ruth Hsiao, and Gwen Romagnoli, who were writing colleagues when I first considered a book about my street. I may never have pursued the project had they not insisted it was worth the effort. Gwen read and edited several chapters near the end, catching factual and copy errors.

My friend Judy Watkins encouraged me from the start — suggesting original sources, visiting archives with me, and editing early, very rough drafts. When I completed all eleven chapters before the the editing process began, three people kindly read the manuscript from start to finish: Jean Gibran, Norma Zack, and South End Historical Society Director, Hope Shannon. I am very grateful for their comments and suggestions.

Anne Smart, Deborah Madrey, and Carol Glass at the Boston Public Library's South End branch helped me track down books on many occasions in order to re-check facts. They saved me hours toward the end of an arduous editing process.

I also wish to thank Ann Hershfang, Ken Kruckemeyer, Mel King, Alison Barnet, Paul Wright, Gene Boehne, and Dan Ocasio who spent additional time clarifying chronologies and events that I was not sure I had represented accurately.

It pleases me enormously to thank Emily Callejas (formerly Emily Potts of Holyoke Street) who read chapters as I wrote them, cheering me on and helping me with the tone of the book. Sam Potts (formerly of Holyoke Street, now of New York City) is the designer who chose everything to do with the visual presentation of the book and helped with the book's production from start to finish. I couldn't have done it without him. As I always say about these two children, "They turned out great."

Last, but never least, I wish to thank Gardiner Hartmann, erstwhile Berkeley graduate student, Vermont farmer, and former husband, who did tireless cutting and pasting, organizing and rearranging on a final draft that I had been close to for too long to know how it read. He was central to the entire endeavor — as he has been to all the good things that have happened in my life.

INDEX

Note: Page numbers in *italics* refer to illustrations.

Made in the USA
Charleston, SC
12 December 2012